#STOLEN

Is Social Media Stealing Your Identity?

JESSICA FRALIN

ABINGDON PRESS
NASHVILLE

Library of Congress Cataloging-in-Publication Data has been requested.

Fralin, Jessica.
  #Stolen : is social media stealing your identity? / Jessica Fralin.
     pages cm
  Includes bibliographical references.
     ISBN 978-1-4267-8906-9 (binding: soft back) 1. Social media—Religious aspects—Christianity. 2. Social media addiction. 3. Self-esteem in women—Religious aspects—Christianity. 4. Identity (Psychology)—Religious aspects—Christianity. 5. Internet and women—Psychological aspects. 6. Internet and youth—Psychological aspects. 7. Internet addiction—Religious aspects—Christianity. I. Title.
  BV4596.I57F73 2015
  261.5'2—dc23

                                                                                     2015014541

15 16 17 18 19 20 21 22 23 24—10 9 8 7 6 5 4 3 2 1
MANUFACTURED IN THE UNITED STATES OF AMERICA

#STOLEN

To Drew, Taylor, Anna, Kayleigh, Makayla and Sierra:
You sparked the idea for this book without even knowing it.
I love you all so much.

CONTENTS

WORDS, WORDS, WORDS

REDEEMING OUR TIME (& OUR TWEETS)

WHAT'S THE PROBLEM?

When I started high school, smartphones were just a blip on the radar—something only the really tech-savvy (or really rich!) were talking about. I had a Facebook account, but that was my only social media outlet. And I could only log in from my home computer!

Walking through the halls of high school each year, I literally watched a transformation take place. Social media grew. Phones got smarter. We could make purchases, plans, and even friends without any face-to-face interaction. Managing status updates and online profiles grew from a hobby into an entire way of doing life. This was not the world our parents grew up in!

As this tech revolution took place, we had more information than ever before, and we had more ways to connect to it. And it was all a lot of fun. But honestly? Underneath all the hype there were problems growing, too. Social media has smashed into the center of our lives, and it's here to stay. That's why I'm writing a whole book about it. The way we handle it matters.

Whether we are on our computers, iPads, or smartphones, we love to spend time on social media and talk about it. Maybe you've even used one site to talk about what's going on with another site. In many ways, social media runs our world.

But what if it's also trying to run us?

Think about the Harlem Shake, for example. In what other society could that craze have ever happened? A bunch of people wearing weird outfits and dancing when the beat drops, then putting it online for the world to see? And then a bunch more of us saying, "Sounds cool. Let's do it. Maybe our video will go viral!" And no one even questions it.

Trust me, I'm not against the Harlem Shake. I participated in one of said videos alongside thousands of other people at my university, and it was a blast. I just think it says a lot about us.

Social media says, "Jump!" and we all say, "How high?" It sets the standards—telling us what's pretty, what's acceptable, even what's morally right and wrong. If we let it, it will even tell us who we are. The time you spend scrolling and swiping on your screens matters. Every post on social media sends a message—some are true; some are definitely not. Do you ever stop to think about what you're staring at? What messages are you hearing? And are they true?

We often buy into those standards without thinking twice, adjusting our lives accordingly. But do we want social media to have that kind of power in our lives? Do we want to live life by social media's standards—or would we like to set our own?

The problem with being defined by who we are online is that we can control our existence there. We can hide all the messy parts, play up the adventures, and even twist the truth a little when it comes to how well things are going in our lives. But how does it feel when people start holding us up to this unrealistic standard? What happens when we start to give other people identities based on their curated, on-screen selves? Here's the bottom line when it comes to social media: who we are online isn't who we really are.

Our cute little put-together lives are fake, and we all know it. Sometimes life is messy, or we are hurting. Sometimes we have needs that can't be met through a screen. Sometimes we have bad days, or sad days, days when we don't feel good enough. How can we work through those hurts if we're always trying to cover them up? We have to dive deep into that mess if we want to be healed from it. When we settle for the filtered, 140-character versions of ourselves, we're going to end up losing who we really are.

I love social media and I want you to love it, too. But I know from personal experience that it will try to steal who you really are. For better and worse, social media plays a big part in your life. But the lies out there don't have to. If you've ever felt empty after posting an edited selfie, lonely for real relationships even as your follower count goes up, or frustrated about trying to sort out the difference between who your Instagram bio says you are and what your real life shows, then this is the book for you. It's time to take back what social media has stolen from our true identities. Let's fight for the freedom to be who we really are!

Chapter 1

#STOLEN

How Social Media Has Told Us
Who We Are

This is probably weird, but I like to walk by open laptops in a coffee shop (which is where I spend at least half of my free time). I always peek to see if Facebook, Twitter, or Pinterest is open. Almost every time, at least one of them is. Sometimes all three. And smartphones are everywhere. They've become the Mom-I-really-have-to-have-this gift of the century. It's incredible, isn't it? We get to be connected 24/7, to almost all of the information in the world. (Although my greatest talent when it comes to the iPhone seems to be shattering my screen.) If you're not on Twitter, people question your sanity, because *everybody* is on Twitter. Even my grandma has a Twitter account, and she's eighty years old!

It seems like everywhere I turn these days, social media has entered another part of our world. And I'm loving the way it keeps us all connected. But have you ever been annoyed by it? Has it ever made you feel overwhelmed or frustrated? For all the good we can do with it, there are a few things there I wish we could press the "dislike" button for.

LIKE/DISLIKE

Social media and I have a love/hate relationship. I have a lot of thoughts bouncing around in my head, pretty much all the time. Call it "creative type," call it hyperactivity, call it whatever you want, but I have a lot to say. Funny occurrences, insights I've found, stories that need sharing. Social media provides an outlet for all these thoughts, neatly packaged in 140 characters or less and sent to all my followers with one little click. That's the part I love.

But after I click that button, I wait to see how my words will affect my followers. Will they laugh along at the funny things I write? Will my realizations cause them to think deeper too? Sometimes, after I've hit "send," I'm held captive by my notifications. It's a waiting game, not just to see *how* my words will affect my friends, but *if* my words will affect them at all. Part of me fears that after I've put my words out there, the notifications won't come. Social media has trained my heart to believe that notifications are what give my words worth, what gives *me* worth. It might be one of the biggest battles I face when it comes to social media. And that's the part I hate.

It's not just the notifications, though. My love/hate relationship with social media continues in so many ways:

Love: I can stay connected with my friends who live across the country.

Hate: I can look at my friends' posts and feel jealous that their lives are cooler than mine.

Love: I can find killer ideas for everything from outfits to room decor to recipes.

Hate: I sometimes feel like I'll never measure up to the ideas I find.

Love: I can read a Tweet or a blog and immediately feel encouraged and excited.

Hate: I can read a Tweet or a blog and immediately feel disappointed and defeated.

Love: I can be connected to everyone's thoughts, all the time.

Hate: I can't stop waiting for everyone to validate my own thoughts that I post online.

I could go on and on, but I'm sure you get the picture. If any of those scenarios resonates in your life, take heart, friend. I can assure you, you are not alone. I'm all too familiar with the highs and lows social media can bring into your life.

#ADDICTED

There was a time when I allowed social media to build me up and tear me down. I let it decide what was important about me, to define me, to tell me who I was. The incessant chatter on my millions of accounts (OK, maybe just twelve, but it *feels* like millions) slowly crept into my life over time and dug deep roots. I became addicted. And for the longest time, I didn't even realize it. I thought I could quit letting social media control me any time I wanted. But you know what? That was an absolute lie. The first time I tried to take a break from Twitter, I think I lasted four hours. *Four hours.* Yikes. Can anyone say "addicted"?

What do you think would happen if you gave up your cell phone for an entire day? What would be the hardest part? What might be good about it?
#GiveItATry

•••

Addiction is a word running wild today. It's splashed across headlines and rolls off the tongues of news broadcasters. You've heard the tragic stories about celebrities and next-door neighbors alike who got sucked in by a problem they never dreamed they'd have. Some people are held captive by drugs or alcohol, while others are consumed with shopping or eating or gambling. Whatever their obsessions, you've learned to recognize addiction in people. You've learned to recite the maxim "everything in moderation," and maybe even started to tune out the endless talks you get in classrooms and on commercials about the dangers these things can cause. All the while, some of us are busy feeding our own obsession with pinning and liking and commenting every day. It seems innocent enough, doesn't it? But could this be a whole new brand of addiction—one that's subtle and socially acceptable?

It's dangerous because we live in the loudest time in history. The voices are constant, and there are so many of them. Even in our most silent moments, we allow a multitude of voices in, letting them speak deep statements in our lives—statements about who we are, what we are worth, and who we should measure ourselves against. Words bombard us all the time. Comparisons. Criticisms. Compliments. And we don't even have to speak to anyone to hear them. Do you think maybe we've become addicted to the noise?

All too often, I've let the chatter become my measuring stick. I let all those voices on social media define me. I crave validation from them and feel depressed when I don't get it. Does that sound familiar to you? If so, I'm glad you picked up this book. Turning the chatter off and tuning it out are two of the hardest things I've ever learned, but they are also the most rewarding. I'm excited to dive in with you and explore how we can do that in the world of social media. I may not know you in real life—I don't follow you on Twitter or have coffee with you every other weekend—but I feel like I do know you in a small way because we're hanging out in this social-media–dominated world together. And we all hurt the same when our identities get stolen by this "little" addiction. It's worth the effort to fight this obsession: your heart matters way too much to let social media tell you who you are.

#FACTCHAT

So what's this FactChat section all about? Well, there are a ton of statistics, facts, and figures thrown around when it comes to social media. But what does it really mean for you? In each chapter, I'm going to give you some interesting research or news to think about. And *you'll also see a few questions to help you sort through why it matters. You can reflect on these anecdotes alone or, better yet, chat about them with your friends or discuss them at your next youth group meeting.*

* * *

A professor at Oxford University has determined that 150 is about the maximum number of friendships the human brain can handle. So what does that mean for all those people with thousands of Facebook friends? When he studied the actual traffic on Facebook sites, he discovered that most people only maintain an inner circle of about 150 relationships in the online world as well.

- *What's the difference between friends and followers?*
- *Do you think the number of followers someone has on social media makes a difference in how they live real life?*
- *How does social media help you maintain friendships?*

(www.dailymail.co.uk/news/article-1245684/5-000 -friends-Facebook-Scientists-prove-150-cope-with.html)

PROTECTING YOUR IDENTITY

This social media problem is a two-in-one deal. On the surface, there's the problem of dealing with the noise. Maybe you've just become immune to it. You expect it, and maybe even crave it. (Stay tuned for the next chapter, because it has a lot to say about how that noisiness affects your life.) But there's a deeper problem underneath all the chatter. It's not just that you *have* voices constantly speaking to you. The problem is that those voices will try to *define* you.

I'm sure it stinks to have your financial identity stolen, but I don't know a thing about it. The kind of identity theft I'm passionate about preventing can't be found in a serial number or a bank account. Your identity is far more complex and cool than that, because it's intangible. It's in your heart and your soul. It's been carefully crafted. It's one of a kind. Do you know who you really are? You've already been defined. As beautiful. As unique. As loved.

Don't let social media tell you any different. Somehow, simply being human seems to walk hand in hand with insecurity. It's weirdly comforting to know that this struggle is universal: no age, gender, race, or financial situation is immune to the insecurities that can wreck us. We all struggle to know the truth about who we are—and even more so, to believe it. There's something deep within us that craves security, love, and worth—we're wired for it. Just glance back through your history books and you'll see that in every generation, humans have been desperate for these things. And you'll also see that people have always struggled to believe that they are good enough, loved enough, and beautiful enough. The lies that whisper to your soul didn't pop up out of nowhere. It's a struggle that's existed from the first recorded days and continues as you're reading this page.

But while this isn't just a "your generation" or "your gender" problem, your search for significance and acceptance does show up in a unique way. Before we dive any deeper into this book, I want to reassure you of something.

Your desire to be loved is okay.

Cling to that truth. Hold it tight when you hear those incessant voices whisper things like, "You don't need anything. Or anyone. Just be independent." Maybe you've listened to those whispers and tried to silence those needs, to become self-sufficient and independent and strong. I've sure tried before. But I learned that it doesn't work. Because it isn't supposed to. Our desire to be loved is more than okay—it's part of what makes us human. Take a moment and let that truth sink in.

Of course, sometimes we fight that truth because it hurts a lot when that desire for love is unmet. But what if that desire was woven into your soul by someone who already desires *you?* What if it really is possible to be satisfied and whole? Isn't this exactly what every generation has longed for? Maybe reading the words on these pages has caused something in the secret parts of your heart to sigh with relief that you are not alone in this. Maybe there's been a vague, dull emptiness in you, and you just can't put your finger on why. Maybe you're restless or discontent or tired. I know how you feel, because I've felt it, too.

We're all walking through this together. Every girl, for all of time, has walked through those voices that cry out to define us, to stamp value on us, to compare us to one another. But even though that's true, you and I are standing on a new battleground today. Because our generation is up against voices that scream louder and more often than ever before.

#FACTCHAT

According to recent data, the average American smartphone user has downloaded 32.8 apps to a device. Want to guess the most downloaded app? If you said Facebook, you're right. A whopping 76.1 percent of us have that app on our phones.

- *How many apps do you have on your phone? How many of those connect you to social media?*
- *What kind of information do these apps help you share with the online world?*
- *What kind of apps help you "edit" the version of yourself you put online? What kind of things do people try to hide on social media? What kind of things do they tend to show off?*

(http://mashable.com/2013/09/05/most-apps-download -countries/. Also see http://mashable.com/2013/09/12 /popular-smartphone-apps/)

LIFE BEFORE SNAPCHAT

Just think for a minute about the voices that influenced generations in the past. Before social media, your options to communicate hurtful words or gossip were limited. You could use your home telephone to call the other person's home telephone, which another member of their family might easily answer instead. If that felt too risky, maybe you could write out your rant and send it in a letter. Yes, an actual letter—a piece of paper that takes several days to get delivered to a mailbox. Or, if you were patient, you could just wait to talk to your friend in person.

How many of the comments that you see online every day would actually make it if they had to go through one of these options instead?

How about comparing your beauty to others? Before the Internet, you could go to the store and buy a magazine. You could flip through the few local channels you have on your television. Or you could go to the mall and look at what other girls were wearing and shopping for.

What about getting to know what the cute guy in your class was up to? Well, that's too bad. Unless you knew one of his friends who would tell you all about his life, or you creepily followed him around, you would just have to *actually get to know him*. Oh, the horror. Can you imagine?

I know that all sounds archaic to you. But your parents and grandparents actually conducted their lives that way. And the further back you look, the fewer voices each generation before you heard. Today, our lives are filled with voices that teenagers years ago never even dreamed of.

Today, if you have something hurtful to say, you can post it, text it, Tweet it, or better yet, subtweet it. The options are endless.

Comparisons? Just hop on Pinterest. Or Tumblr. Check out any fashion blog or store website. TiVo any reality show. Everywhere you turn, you find the world's standards of fashion and beauty staring you right in the face.

And that cute boy? You can just follow him—not in real life, but on Facebook, Twitter, Instagram. Almost every personal detail of his life will be available to you. You can decide whether you're "in love" or not before you even speak a word to him.

That's the world we live in. But can you see how dangerous it can be? We can spend so much of our lives staring and comparing on social media that we start to view the world through that little screen. We start to view the truth that way. We let the voices of social media define us. I've seen it happen. And I hope you see it, too. When we realize that our identities have truly been stolen, we'll start to fight to get them back.

Can I tell you something? Your life is interesting. *You* are interesting! Your life is so much more beautiful and complex and wild and wonderful than you could ever fit into 140 characters. You know that Dr. Seuss line, "There is no one alive who is youer than you?" I know you're way past nursery rhymes, but there's actually a lot of truth in that silly little sentence. You weren't created to live just like everyone else. Comparison is a game we were never wired to play. But when you neglect your real life for the manicured one you present on social media, you start to become that online persona instead of the real person you are. Do you really think the number of favorites you got on your last Tweet matters very much? Do you really think the girl whose Tweet has one star beside it is worth less than the girl who just reached 500 of them? I'll bet both of them have a unique and wonderful life to live, regardless of what Twitter has to say. Social media doesn't define you.

Unless you let it.

That brings us back to the truth bomb I dropped on you a couple pages ago: Your desire to be loved is okay. And you don't need to deny that need. Your job is to find out *where* you were designed to have that need met. There's a way to fill all those voids and insecurities. There's a way to enjoy social media without letting it steal your identity. I'm living in the reality of it. And I want you to live in that reality with me. But it's not easy.

To get to the truth, we have to stomp out all the lies that we've believed, both the obvious ones and the subtle ones. It's tough, but it's worth it. Are you ready?

FIGHTING FIRES

Let's think about social media lies as fires. Not the innocent campfire kind. The lies of social media are unwanted and dangerous fires, and they have to be put out *right now*. As you read this book, some of the pieces that social media has stolen from your heart will become clear to you. When it comes to those, we can just take a bucket of water and drown them out in the blink of an eye. But some of those lies will be sneaky. Some lies you might not even see at first, like embers from a fire that land on your skin and glow for a moment before you even realize they burn. Left unattended, though, one of those embers can burn through a whole forest. All of us have been burned in one way or another by the identity games of social media. So we have to search for those hidden lies that are hurting us. And we have to put those out, too.

#FACTCHAT

Could a cell phone literally start a fire? It happened in Texas when a thirteen-year-old girl woke up to a smoldering cell phone under her pillow! The cause? An overheating battery.
(http://myfox8.com/2014/07/25/samsung-phone
-catches-fire-under-girls-pillow/)

Putting out fires is never easy. I can't promise you that insecurities and lies will stop trying to wage war on your heart after you finish this book. But I can promise that you'll know where to turn when you need to fight them. There's freedom and victory to be found on the other side of our stolen identities.

Just picture a forest after a fire. Even after the most devastating fires, something crazy happens. Growth. Growth in insane proportions. All the burned pieces create rich soil that's ready to house new plants. The dead has been burned away, and new, green life explodes everywhere you look. I think our hearts can look like that—full of new life. When we stop letting social media tell us who we are, we're free to find our identities in all the right places. And as someone who has experienced both the devastation and the new life, I know it's worth it.

Years ago, I heard the phrase "you are better healed than well," and it really bothered me. I didn't want to be healed from anything because I didn't want to be sick. None of us chooses to be sick, do we? And I'm not just talking about physical sickness. I don't think anyone wants to see sickness in their lives emotionally, spiritually, or mentally. But after walking through some battles and gaining some wisdom along the way, I've come to love that quote. I cling to it. I rest in it. Because now that I've learned to stare into the face of my sickness, I understand what victory looks like. And I've learned what love looks like because I've been loved even at my darkest.

And so have you. You are loved. Do you believe that? I hope and pray that you will by the end of this book, because it's a truth that will set you free.

> *Examine me, God! Look at my heart!*
> *Put me to the test! Know my anxious thoughts!*
> *Look to see if there is any idolatrous way in me,*
> *then lead me on the eternal path!*
> —Psalm 139:23-24

IDENTITY: TAKING IT BACK

It's easy to read words on a page. It's harder to apply those words to your heart. But without asking the hard questions, we won't ever get our identities back. So at the end of each chapter, I'm going to ask you a few questions. They might seem easy to answer at first. But once you answer them, I encourage you to act, to start believing truth in place of lies. Take some time to search your heart for the lies that you've been believing. You have to know what fires are burning before you start to fight them.

1. We have to see where we are weak before we can learn how to be strong. If you are honest with yourself, what insecurity would you say fights for your heart most often? Are there voices that feed it? If so, which ones?

2. Is your heart feeling restless, listless, or just a little bit empty? What have you been trying to fill it with? Is it working?

Chapter 2

10 PERCENT REMAINING

Sucking the Life Out of More
Than Just Your Battery

20,000. That's a big number. Twenty thousand people couldn't even fit into my hometown's football stadium. Twenty thousand days adds up to more than fifty-four years. And $20,000? Can you imagine what'd you do with that much money? I could pay my rent for the year and still fly to Hawaii for a few weeks.

No matter what it's referring to, 20,000 is a lot. So apparently we girls have a lot to say.

It has been said that women use 20,000 words every day. *Every day!* I'd say we were created for conversation, wouldn't you?

Community is a really cool thing. And how do you build it? With words and with time. Just think about it: how do you form friendships? You talk to someone. You spend time with them. It's really not a complicated equation, and it's been going on since the beginning of time. Things like transportation, architecture, and even fashion have been transformed time and again. But the way

> **#FACTCHAT**
> *According to Nielsen Company tracking, in 2011 women talked on cell phones for 818 minutes per month compared to 640 minutes by men. The female/male text ratio was 716 to 555.*
> *(www.emirates247.com/lifestyle/it-s-official-women-talk-text-more-than-men-2011-12-26-1.434582)*

we build relationships has pretty much remained intact with those two simple ingredients: words and time.

But then, along came social media, and things changed in a really big way.

GAME CHANGER

Social media is a game changer for relationships, both in practicality and in matters of the heart. But don't read the word *change* and immediately think *negative*. Some people out there have a panicked mentality about social media. You've probably met them. They say things like, "Social media is horrible! Run from it as fast as you can!" I'm not one of those people. Screaming that opinion from the rooftops would just make me a hypocrite and someone who's totally out of touch. Truth is, I love social media. That's why I've had to fight being addicted to it. Sadly, there's potential for a lot of bad on social media. But there's also a huge potential for good, and I wouldn't want us to miss that.

I'd never suggest you delete all your accounts and become a hermit. Because I'd never do it either. But I do want to shed light on the ugly side of social media, not because I'm a killjoy, but *so that you can fight it*. I don't want you to feel defeated all the time by the lies social media whispers—and sometimes screams. Life is so much better when you gain victory over those deceptions: I know because I've experienced that change for myself.

Social media is a game changer for relationships, yes. But we can make it one for the better. And there's a lot of good to be found. After all, it is *social* media. And we can use it for building relationships rather than causing isolation and insecurity.

GENERATION IMMEDIATE

So how exactly has social media changed relationships? Well, in the past, words and time may have been the only two things required for building friendships, but they were both required. Every time. Relationships couldn't really grow unless you talked to people, and that required spending time with them.

That equation is getting flipped on its head today. We live in the generation of "immediate." Time is something that we just don't want to spend anymore, on anything. When we're hungry, we put things in the microwave, because cooking from scratch takes way too long. When we need a new dress or a textbook for class, we buy it online. Going out to shop? Nah. We don't have time for that. Sometimes I'll find myself clicking on a link expecting to find an article I can skim, but instead I'm directed to a video that's five minutes long. And I'll decide I don't care enough to watch.

Because goodness knows I'm way too busy for a five-minute video. Can you relate?

We're the generation of immediate gratification. And even though microwaves and online shopping aren't bad things, the mind-set that comes along with them can be. In our culture of instant everything, we desire immediate satisfaction across the board, even when it comes to people. But have you ever met a person who works that way? You can't just snap your fingers and end up with a lifelong friend. People aren't wired like that. Relationships take words and time. And then some more words. And some more time.

Now, remember that "20,000 words" statistic I mentioned earlier? Words clearly aren't the part of the equation that we find difficult. We have a lot to say, and social media gives us a louder voice than ever before. All that chatter we've been talking about? Your voice is a part of it. You have an audience. You get to make an impact. No, words aren't going anywhere. As girls, I think we'll always be okay with the "talking" part of the friendship equation.

The problem we have today? It's with time.

Today's "instant" lifestyle often replaces quality time with "quick fixes." Between iMessages and Snapchats and favorited Tweets, we are in constant contact with people. We're connected all the time. We have hundreds of social media "friends." You may have people who are curious about your life, interested in what happens in your day to day, and listening to the words you type. You may have tons of followers on Twitter, Tumblr, or Instagram. But followers and friends are not really the same thing.

We're the most connected generation in all of history. We are also the loneliest. Do you think that's a coincidence?

Some people suggest that young people who've grown up doing a lot of "talking" via social media aren't able to carry on good conversations in real life. Others argue that meaningful conversations can happen on social media, too. #WhatDoYouThink?

• • •

Studies show that as we spend more time typing words on a screen, we spend less time engaging in face-to-face conversations with those around us. Social media enables us to read one another's monologues, close the laptop, and move on unchanged. We lose the art of dialogue, the back and forth of personal conversations. We type and post and click, hoping to be heard, but so does everyone else. Is anyone really listening? All too often, the more we "talk" on social media, the lonelier we feel. We will never be satisfied when we replace deep friendships, encouraging words, and quality time with character-restricted sentences and button-click affirmations. We spend so much of our time staring at screens. Are we missing out on honest conversation and genuine community right around us?

TAKING THE TIME

Of course, it sounds crazy to choose the quick-fix relationships of social media over having real-life friends. But most of us have done it at times, haven't we? Why? I think it's because relationships are hard. Life is messy, as I'm sure you already know. Some days, it feels like I go through every single emotion. Sometimes twice. Some areas of life just aren't as black and white as I want them to be. And sometimes I don't even understand myself, much less other people.

So adding those other people into this equation is tough. It means sacrificing my need to be understood and trying to understand them. It means putting my burdens on a shelf sometimes so I can help them carry theirs. It means seeking to be more of a listener and less of a talker. And when I do talk, I have to offer encouraging, kind, and loving words, not words that will tear other people down or defeat their hearts. With real-life friendships, I have to invest my time. Time I might prefer to spend watching *The Voice* or taking a nap or reading. Basically, it comes down to this: if I want to live in genuine community, it can't be all about me.

I guess even in a social media–dominated world, the equation hasn't *really* changed. Life-giving words and sacrificial time: isn't that what you crave from people? That's still what it takes for us to do life with one another.

But are we too busy Tweeting about our feelings to remember what it's like to sit across the table from someone who's actually listening? Are we so busy posting selfies, dying for someone to tell us we're beautiful, that we forget that the hearts of other girls need to hear those words too? Sometimes I worry that we're all carefully crafting our profiles but forgetting to carefully craft our character.

And it's sucking the life right out of us.

#FACTCHAT

A University of Michigan psychologist tracked Ann Arbor residents for five days by text messages, asking about their Facebook use, their amount of personal interactions, and their overall feelings. What did he learn? The more time people spent on Facebook between texts, the less happy and satisfied they felt. Another study dug deeper and looked at what people were doing on Facebook. Their discovery? When people were passive consumers of Facebook, their feelings of loneliness increased, but those who were actively posting on walls, "liking" updates, and messaging others felt their loneliness decrease.

- Why do you think social media use causes many people to feel depressed or dissatisfied?
- Why do you think being an active user versus a passive consumer makes such a big difference in how people feel about their social media use?
- What kind of things can you do to be active in your social media relationships?

(www.newyorker.com/tech/elements/how-facebook
-makes-us-unhappy)

I know this is a lot of real talk in a few short pages. It's tough looking in the mirror and seeing that addiction has robbed us of community. It would be easier to look back at our smartphones and return to business as usual. But what are you actually looking *for* when you turn to social media?

So much of our activity on social media is a cry for affirmation, for love, for community. But here's the irony. When we spend all of our time looking for community on social media, while rejecting the real community around us, it makes us even emptier. And so where do we turn? Back to social media. It's a vicious cycle, and it's draining us. When I was stuck in it, I was drained faster than my iPhone battery. I felt like I had 10 percent remaining on my joy in life, all because I ran to social media to find my friendships and my worth.

Social media can be great. It's a great way to connect with the friends I may not see very often. It's a great way for me to influence the audience I have for good. It's a great tool for lots of things. But there should be conditions. Social media can never take the place of genuine community. It can never be the place I draw my sense of worth from. When I look to social media as my source of life, I end up missing out and burning out.

I don't want my life to be drained by this thing that can be so good.

GOOD TO BETTER

The truth of it is we turn good things into bad things when we try to make them the *best* thing. And when it comes to your heart, it was designed for Jesus to be that best thing. When we put our possessions, our hobbies, our relationships, or our online presence into that "best thing" position, things go south—and fast! Should we love social media? Yes! I think it's one of the coolest parts of the world we live in. But should we love it more than we love Jesus? No way. I've learned that if we really want to enjoy social media—and not end up feeling drained by it—we just need to give it the proper place in our heart. And while we don't need to run *from* anything, there are definitely a few things we should be running *to*.

RUN TOWARD COMMUNITY

Maybe the term *community* doesn't make a ton of sense to you. That's okay. All I mean is that not everyone you interact with is building healthy and encouraging relationships with you, so be careful to seek out genuine people every chance you get. When I think of the friends I hold closest in my heart, the people I want to do life with day in and day out, there are a few characteristics that come to mind. Hopefully this will help you recognize real community in your own life.

COMMUNITY IS HONEST

As girls, we've all seen plenty of fake in our lives, haven't we? False pretenses block the way to real community. So build relationships with people who are going to be honest with you. You need people who will tell you when you're in the wrong but who also will be the first ones to build you up when you're doing things right. You need people who will tell you what you need to hear instead of what you want to hear. But they say it because they love you. These are real friends. They are on your side, and they're loyal enough not to lie to you. Find honest community—and be ready to be honest yourself.

COMMUNITY IS CONSISTENT

We all have those friends who flit in and out of our lives whenever it's convenient for them. Doesn't make us feel very valued, does it? If we want to find genuine community, we need to search for people who will be around on our best days *and* our worst ones. If people don't take the time to be around us, how can they understand us, love us, or be honest with us? Pick people who will be there when things get rough, and try to be there for them through their highs and lows as well.

COMMUNITY IS SACRIFICIAL

Have you ever noticed how inconvenient friendship can be? Sometimes I just don't feel like being a good friend. I don't want to hear the same story for the eighty-seventh time or drive someone to the airport before the sun comes up or grab coffee with a friend when my budget is barely scraping by. But you know what? Real friends do that stuff anyway. Anybody can give you a Twitter shout-out. Only a real friend will make a sacrifice for you. In real community, people are there for you with their actions, not just with their words. Of course, that means you're going to have to take one for the team sometimes, too. Actually, you'll probably have to take a lot for the team. But so will your friend. And that kind of sacrifice will make you closer than you could've dreamed.

Finding people who are honest, consistent, and sacrificial may not be easy. But I can't encourage you enough to keep searching for them. You know what's so special about those traits? People who are willing to do those things are people who really love you. And those kinds of relationships fill you up instead of sucking you dry. And once you've found that real community? Take it to social media. That's right. Blow up Twitter and Instagram with the encouraging words and awesome experiences that will inevitably happen when you're doing life with people. It's so much fun, and it's so fulfilling. I promise.

What would be different if you made your next "comment"
to a friend in person instead of on a social media site?
#GiveItATry

•••

RUN TOWARD TRUTH

Do you know what truth looks like? We live in this world where everyone has his or her opinion, and sometimes it seems like a million different ones are flying around us all at once. Lots of people believe that no one is really right or wrong, and we can all just believe whatever we want. That's confusing, and a little bit scary. In a world full of all these different thoughts and beliefs and opinions, is there really something that's flat-out *true*? I believe there is. All this talk about social media not being able to define us because we've already been defined as loved and beautiful and valued? Yeah, you might have thought I was crazy. Or wondered where I was getting that information. Or been confused about how I could possibly know that about *you*, since I've (most likely) never had the privilege of meeting you. Well, I'm getting my information from a very reliable source. I've experienced truth that has changed every piece of my heart and every part of my crazy life. And it's found in the Bible.

Maybe you grew up like me, in a home where your family believed the Bible. From the time I was in preschool, I grew up reading Bible stories and knowing all about who God is and how much He loves me. But as I grew up, a disconnect started forming between the things I knew in my head and the things I believed in my heart. My head knew that God loved me and thought I was beautiful. But I let some of the incessant chatter of the world make me feel like I wasn't. I let those opinions filter into my heart rather than running toward truth. Over time, I figured something out: truth doesn't have to do with how I feel. I'm a girl—I feel 957 different ways in a single day! But truth is just true, no matter how I'm feeling. I am loved and beautiful and valued. No ifs, ands, or buts about it.

Of course, maybe your story is nothing like mine. Perhaps you've never read the Bible or heard that God loves you. Or maybe you've heard about it once or twice, but you've never really considered that it could be true. I'm asking you right now to consider, what if it *is* true? What if you are truly loved and beautiful and valued by God?

I want to jump up and down on the couch I'm sitting on right now, because I know beyond a shadow of a doubt that it *is* the truth! And it's the most exciting truth I've ever found. If you're not sure what to think about this God yet or you're not really convinced that He thinks you're beautiful and valued and loved, that's okay. I hope you'll keep walking with me down this road to freedom from our stolen identities. And along the way, I'll tell you more about why He gets to define the truth—and how that truth has changed my life completely for the better.

But no matter where you are with God right now, I hope you'll run toward truth. Look for real answers, not the touched-up ones social media tries to sell. Pick up the Bible and read a little bit of it, whether you've read it a thousand times or never before. If you run toward the chatter, you will drown in the chaos of opinions and overwhelming noise, and it will suck the life right out of you. But if you run toward truth, you'll find a quiet place to rest and be filled up again.

And isn't that what you've been craving all along?

"Then you will know the truth, and the truth will set you free."
—John 8:32

IDENTITY: TAKING IT BACK

1. Some people say our generation is so addicted to conversations on our phones that we can't hold conversations in real life. Does the idea of real-life community scare you?

2. Which is hardest for you: honesty, consistency, or sacrifice? How do you think adding that to your friendships, even when it's hard, would change them?

THE COMPARISON GAME

There are a lot of things I don't know about you. Maybe you have freckles across your nose or streaks of hot pink in your hair. You might love high heels; you might love vintage T-shirts. Or you might love both. I don't know your favorite song or ice cream flavor or movie. Or whether you'd rather hang out at the beach or hike up a mountain.

You probably have some quirks, too. I know I do. It bugs me to no end when I step on a wet spot in my kitchen when I have socks on. Maybe your quirk is that you only drink sweet tea on Tuesdays, or that you can't sleep with socks on, or that you can say your ABCs backwards really fast. I don't know, because I don't really know you.

Here's what I do know: there isn't anyone else just like you.

Isn't that awesome? Hanging out with people who are different from me is one of my favorite things. And I'm sure I'd love getting to know you, too. We could grab a snack and laugh about all those little quirks and maybe bond over our love of boy bands or cinnamon lattes or handwritten letters, if you love those things. If you don't, we'd celebrate all the cool things you love, too. Different is cool. And I always learn a lot.

Unfortunately, somewhere along the way, our world has forgotten how to celebrate "different." Social media has sped up the process of discouraging individuality and encouraging conformity instead. Subtly but powerfully, our lives have been turned into one big comparison. As we scroll down our screens, we compare our bodies, our personalities, and our stuff to no end. It's just an ongoing game of trying to be enough.

I don't know about you, but I don't think the game is much fun. No one ever seems to win. And I don't want to play it any more.

Wouldn't the world be a better place if we could celebrate one another instead of competing all the time? Do you even believe you are someone worth celebrating? I do, and I can say that confidently, even though we've never met. Want to know why? Read on.

Chapter 3

DOUBLE TAP

When Likes Define Life

I took a sip of my coffee and cringed. It was room temperature. I might just be the world's greatest coffee consumer—I'll drink an iced vanilla latte or a piping hot Americano with equal enthusiasm—but room temperature? Absolutely not. Allowing coffee to go cold is a big deal in my little world. So what caused this terrible turn of events?

I was trying to pick the right filter on Instagram.

Go ahead and laugh. I know it sounds pretty inconsequential. All I missed was a hot cup of coffee. No big deal. But what else have I missed because I was too busy trying to capture and perfect a moment on-screen rather than being present in the moment right in front of me? I've wasted a lot of minutes pulling out my iPhone, documenting whatever experience is happening around me, and then editing it to perfection. I feel this need to get the best lighting, find the most unique angle, and create the funniest hashtag. And even after working so hard to craft this image, I couldn't give you a reason why I took the time.

Now, I realize that capturing moments on camera isn't inherently bad. My camera roll is a journal of sorts, and I have hundreds of great memories stored inside. Instagram is one of my favorite apps. There are some incredibly talented people out there, and I appreciate the art they create on a daily basis. Sometimes I'm so blown away by the beauty I see in creation, or so filled with love for the friends I'm surrounded by, that I simply want to share. And that's the beautiful side of social media—sharing life. But there are also countless times I rob myself of sharing life with the people right in front of me because I'm too busy trying to impress the ones I interact with on social media. I forsake my real life for the one I keep neatly on a four-inch screen.

Is social media turning people into shallow, self-centered narcissists? A recent study showed a direct link between the number of friends someone has on Facebook and his or her score on the Narcissistic Personality Disorder Inventory, noting that narcissists change their profile pics and respond more negatively to comments about themselves on social networking sites. #WhatDoYouThink? (www.theguardian.com/technology/2012/mar/17/face book-dark-side-study-aggressive-narcissism)

•••

TWITTER CALL-OUT

So many of us have thrown real-life moments out the window for the sake of uploading another picture to Instagram. But the problem reaches way beyond Instagram into the world of Tweets, status updates, and Snapchats. Truth is I didn't even see this as a problem until it hit me right between the eyes. I was at a friend's house, sitting at the table after a great meal, halfway participating in the real-life conversation while also checking on my social media life. Suddenly, my friend dropped this bomb into the middle of the conversation and into the depths of my heart: "Hey, Jessica? I really would prefer to hang out with you, and not your Twitter feed."

Okay, I thought. *That was uncalled for on about thirty-seven different levels.* (The sassiness of the voice inside my head is unparalleled.) But I begrudgingly put my phone down and started really listening to the conversation around me for the first time all day. I found out that one of the girls at the table was struggling with her friendships. And I would have just tuned out her pain if I'd kept up my favoriting spree on Twitter. I also laughed until I cried as we shared stories of embarrassing moments and text message blunders. I enjoyed life, right there at that beat-up wooden table, and I enjoyed it way more than my Twitter feed.

That was a catalyst moment in my heart. It's when I started learning what it means to love my real-life moments more than my filtered, 140-character updates. Though I felt a flash of frustration at the initial call-out, in hindsight, I'm thankful beyond words that someone decided to shoot straight with me. Do you have people like that in your life? You need them, sweet friends. I'm amazed at how easily I slide off track in my attitude and priorities without accountability. And for those of us who post, like, and refresh our accounts incessantly, we need those good friends who will keep pulling us back to real life—even when we may not want to hear it.

THRILL OF THE CHASE

Good friends can help you ditch a social media addiction—but you also need a strategy. A few years ago, a very wise lady taught me the strategy of chasing thoughts to their end. Do you ever find yourself circling through the same problems again and again? I know I do. A lot of times, I complain about a problem on the surface but never get to the heart of it. Then I just end up facing that problem over and over and over again. Not fun, is it? So instead of running into the same issues forever, I'm learning to chase my thoughts until I figure out how to change them.

Chase until change.

Catchy phrase, right? But what in the world does it mean? Let's think through an example. Say you can't get to sleep the night before a big test. What do you do? Well, you could drink some Sleepytime tea and count sheep, and maybe that would work. But what if you chased the thoughts instead? Why can't you sleep? Probably because you're nervous for the test. Now keep chasing that thought. You studied for hours and you aced every single flashcard earlier. So why are you still nervous? Well, if you forget the material, you'll fail. So what? (When you ask the "so what?" question, you're usually getting to the end of the chase.) Well, if you fail, that will make you a failure.

And there it is—the end of the thought. You can't sleep because you're afraid you'll be a failure.

Can you see the lie there? Even if you *did* forget all the material and failed the test, it wouldn't make you a failure. It's just one test. But we let ourselves believe lies like this so often, simply because we never chase our thoughts to the end. When the real fear is found, we can call it out and choose to believe the truth instead. And that's exactly what we need to do when we're obsessed with the refresh button on social media.

One day, I checked Twitter three times before there were even any new Tweets in my feed. Does that say obsession? In that moment, I realized that I couldn't chalk my incessant habit up to boredom any longer, and I started the longest and hardest "thought chase" of my life. Why had my mind been wired to constantly favorite Tweets, double tap Instagram pictures, and like Facebook statuses? I was finally honest enough to admit that I felt a need to make my presence known on social media. It wasn't about posting what was really on my mind. It was all about posting things that would warrant the best response from the people who saw it. I chased my thoughts to the end, and do you know what I found? At the heart of my habit was this lie: I was relating my popularity on social media to my worth in real life.

#FACTCHAT

So just how many times can something be Retweeted before Twitter falls apart? The world found out in March 2014, when Ellen DeGeneres Tweeted a selfie with several A-list celebrities at the Oscars. The post garnered more than 2 million Retweets by the end of the evening, blasting *through the previous record held by President Obama. (He garnered more than 780,000 Retweets on his "Four More Years" re-election victory post in November 2012.) The surge in traffic from Ellen's Tweet even knocked out Twitter service for a few minutes!*

- *What are some of the most popular Tweets you've ever seen?*
- *In general, what kind of posts on Twitter tend to get a lot of attention?*
- *What connections do you notice between someone's social media existence and his or her real-life identity? Where do you see big differences between online presence versus reality?*

SO MUCH MORE THAN "LIKED"

If you asked me, "Does the number of likes you get on a profile picture define who you are or how much you're worth?" I would obviously answer no. I knew better, in my mind. But that truth wasn't in the deepest part of my heart. All too often, it *felt* like I was worth more to other people when I was liked online. And when my posts were ignored, I'd get a little down for some reason I couldn't quite put my finger on.

Sound familiar to you? I know I'm not alone in this struggle. The desire to be affirmed, valued, and loved is woven deep into the fabric of your soul. You may spend a lot of your time denying that need. You may spend even more time knowing you have that desire, but trying with all your might to overcome it. Culture tells us that independence is what we should aim for instead. Have you noticed how almost every TV show or movie includes a "needy" or "sensitive" character? The underlying message tells us that feelings and needs make us weak. "Don't be like those annoying characters. Just do what you want and don't try to care about other people. Be the strong, independent character. Those people are free."

This is the message we hear culture telling us at every turn. But can you see how ridiculous it actually is? It might look appealing on screen, but if you take a deeper look, you'll see that even the cultural picture of independence is rooted in insecurities. Because the world also screams that in order to be independent, you must look the best, have the best, and be the most popular. They say you shouldn't have needs, but then they follow up by saying you need all kinds of stuff. Does that make any sense to you? In an effort to show how strong and independent they are, people get stuck in the cycle of trying to one-up each other. And the comparison game keeps driving culture around and around.

Don't you think it's time we stopped playing?

True or False: Women today spend a lot more time comparing each other than affirming each other. #WhatDoYouThink?

●●●

I wish I were sitting across the table from you right now so that I could know your heart, your story, what makes you tick. Our stories always bring our hearts a little closer together, especially as girls. But even as I'm typing these words, there are a few things I already know about you. First, I know that you are loved. That might sound crazy to you. Maybe you still want to roll your eyes and say, "Jessica, you couldn't possibly know that. You don't know about the time when . . ."

But you know what? We all have a "time when." A time when we didn't feel loved. A time when we felt unimportant to the world. A time when we wondered if anyone would ever think we were funny or beautiful or worthy. That's the other thing I know about you: sometimes you don't *feel* loved. I know because I've had all these "time whens," too. I've been the one who didn't get invited to the birthday party, who didn't get the guy, who didn't win the award. And it hurts, doesn't it? But there's good news.

Our "time whens" don't get the last word.

WHO GETS THE LAST WORD?

The last word goes to the One who knew you before time even existed. Someone who knows about every single moment of your life. Everything you love and everything you hate. What color you want to paint your room. What joke makes you laugh every time. Even what you write in every single one of your Tweets.

Maybe that sounds a little scary to you. Because someone who knows *everything* also knows about our messes too, right? He knows about the days when we just don't feel pretty or worthwhile. The ways we work so hard to hide the secrets locked deep in our hearts. He knows how terrified we feel that someone might find it all out. But you know what? The incredibly good news is this: He sees it, and He still loves you.

He's a God who lovingly fashioned you long before you took your first breath. And those desires I mentioned earlier—affirmation, worth, love? He placed those in your heart. They aren't some sort of weakness you need to overcome. You're designed to crave those things for a reason. Do you know what it is? It's because He loves you endlessly. And He wants to fulfill the desires of your heart.

Don't just take my word for it, though. Check out this passage from the book of Psalms so you can see for yourself.

> LORD, *you have examined me.*
>   *You know me.*
> *You know when I sit down and when I stand up.*
>   *Even from far away, you comprehend my plans.*
> *You study my traveling and resting.*
>   *You are thoroughly familiar with all my ways.*
> *There isn't a word on my tongue,* LORD,
>   *that you don't already know completely.*
> *You surround me—front and back.*
>   *You put your hand on me.*
> . . . .
> *You are the one who created my innermost parts;*
>   *you knit me together while I was still in my moth-*
> *er's womb.*
> *I give thanks to you that I was marvelously set apart.*
>   *Your works are wonderful—I know that very well.*
> *My bones weren't hidden from you*
>   *when I was being put together in a secret place,*

*when I was being woven together in the deep parts
of the earth.*
Your eyes saw my embryo,
*   and on your scroll every day was written what was*
being formed for me,
*   before any one of them had yet happened.*
(Psalm 139:1-5, 13-16)

Did you hear what God says about you here? You were made *wonderfully.* God decided before you ever took your first breath that you were beautiful. And you know why He gets to decide? Because He's the one who made you.

Don't rush past this! The God of the entire universe—the One who tells the waves how far they can go and the stars how brightly to shine—He made *you.* Every single piece of you. And every single piece matters to Him—your thoughts, your feelings, and your heart. He wants you to know that His love is enough to quiet all your fears. Enough to silence every insecurity. Enough to end all your striving, trying, and strategizing. You don't have to achieve worth through a screen. And your selfies don't define who you are. No amount of favorited Tweets could ever change the way God feels about you. He's crazy about you.

*Could you post something to Facebook or Twitter and then
go for three days without checking to see if it received comments, likes, or Retweets?
#GiveItATry*

• • •

For a long time, I was crying out for affirmation on social media because I'd forgotten just how cherished and valued I already was. Have you forgotten too? If so, I hope this chapter has been a sweet reminder of the fact that your every word, thought, and movement matters to God. Or maybe you haven't forgotten at all. Maybe you just never knew. If that's you, I'm so glad you picked up this book. And I hope you're ready to learn more about Him, and how He can help you navigate this crazy world of social media.

If you walk away from this chapter only remembering one thing, let it be this: your "likes" do not define your life. You don't have to worry if what you post is good enough or pretty enough or funny enough. Your worth has already been determined, and you are more valuable than you could ever imagine. If you want to play with Instagram filters for thirty minutes at a time, join the club. I still do. Just scroll through them in full confidence, knowing that whether your picture gets one like or one million, you are so loved.

And don't forget to drink your coffee before it gets cold.

> *I give thanks to you that I was marvelously set apart.*
> *Your works are wonderful—I know that very well.*
> —Psalm 139:14

IDENTITY: TAKING IT BACK

1. Where do your "likes" matter most? Your Facebook profile picture, funny Tweets, creative work you post on Instagram, something else?

2. Do you believe any lies about your worth based on your social media statistics? Maybe you compare yourself to others and think you aren't funny or pretty or talented enough. Write it down. Sometimes we don't recognize the lie until we see it. So after you write down the lies, cross them out and replace them with this: "I am _____ enough, because I am fearfully and wonderfully made."

Chapter 4

SELFIES AND SPRAY TANS

When Our Bodies Become Our Gods

It's a trend that changed the Internet forever, especially for us girls. No matter what site you're on, you can find it. Some people are even addicted to it. It would have been unheard of ten years ago, but it's socially acceptable to participate in it today. So acceptable, in fact, that the word has been added to our dictionary. It's easy to do, easy to post, and easy to look for approval from. I'm sure you already know exactly what I'm talking about: the rise of the selfie.

What is it about taking a picture of our faces and sharing it with the world that captivates us so much? Is it a cry for affirmation, like we discussed in the last chapter? I think that explains part of it. But I think the selfie trend reveals a struggle that may be even harder to conquer. Have you noticed what's grown right alongside the rise of the selfie? It's self-obsession. And we all smile and nod and think it's just fine.

But it isn't.

#FACTCHAT

*Even monkeys take selfies—and they can't be copyrighted! In August 2014, a picture taken by an Indonesian macaque went viral, sparking an unsuccessful lawsuit when the camera owner attempted to copyright the image.
(www.theguardian.com/technology/2014/aug/22/monkey-business-macaque-selfie-cant-be-copyrighted-say-us-and-uk)*

It's so easy to fall into the trap of exalting our physical selves above everything else. When we become obsessed with being the skinniest, prettiest, or most fashionable, we allow our bodies to become our gods. And I think they make pretty lousy gods compared to One who actually made us, don't you? But this selfie craze is so new. I don't think that teenagers in the Bible worried about front-facing camera lighting and perfect captions. Can we really find wisdom and truth about this trend within the pages of a book that was written so long ago?

Absolutely.

BRAIDS AND BLING

I'm learning that the Bible really does speak to every issue that I face. You might think God's word is a book about the past, a history lesson of sorts. In a way, you're right. But it's so much more than that. It's also a love letter, a weapon against lies, and a way that God can actively speak to *you*. Today. The words *social media* may not be mentioned in the pages of the Bible, but Jesus knew it would be one of the most important facets of our lives right now. (Remember the psalm we read in the last chapter? He knows every one of our thoughts and has marked all our days.) Smartphones might be new, but human insecurities are not. The Bible is packed full of wisdom about facing insecurity and finding your real identity. And that wisdom doesn't change. It applies just as much to you today as it did to the teenager who was alive while it was written.

Selfies and spray tans would have been a foreign concept to the Apostle Peter. But the idea of beauty was something he certainly saw as important. In fact, he wrote about it in a letter to some Christians who lived in his day. He had some pretty concrete ideas about what beauty is and what it is not. Some of his words might actually shock you a little bit. Check out what 1 Peter 3:3-4 says: "Don't try to make yourselves beautiful on the outside, with stylish hair or by wearing gold jewelry or fine clothes. Instead, make yourselves beautiful on the inside, in your hearts, with the enduring quality of a gentle, peaceful spirit. This type of beauty is very precious in God's eyes."

I can imagine dozens of thoughts running through your mind as you read this. "Side braids make my life so much easier. How dare he tell me to give them up?" "I don't even wear gold jewelry, so this verse doesn't apply to me." "I might have nice clothes, but there was a great sale, so it's fine." Thoughts like this ran through my head when I first read those verses, too. If you have a burning desire to ignore this verse, I don't think you're alone. In fact, for centuries, a lot of people have tried to disregard this verse by explaining that Peter was talking only to the women in Bible times. They argue that this verse just doesn't hold any weight in our culture today. Different culture. Different time. Different rules.

Sure would be nice if we could just agree to move on at this point, right?

But even though I'm the first to stand up for side braids and the way they make life a lot easier on rushed mornings, I believe that Peter's message absolutely applies to you and me today. At the heart of this verse, Peter isn't against hairstyles or clothing or jewelry. Do you see anywhere in this passage where it tells us to run screaming from the world of fashion? No. What Peter does say is this: your beauty shouldn't come from those things.

#FACTCHAT

When fifteen-year-old Danny Bowman took his first selfie, he had no idea how this act would overtake his life. By the age of nineteen, the British teen had become obsessed, spending up to ten hours a day taking more than two hundred selfies. He dropped out of school, lost thirty pounds, and isolated himself for six months in fear that people would notice his imperfections. When he couldn't succeed in capturing a perfect shot, he attempted suicide. Thankfully, the overdose failed, and he went on to receive treatment for technology addiction and a condition called Body Dysmorphic Disorder.
• Why do people take selfies?

- *This is an extreme example, but can you see other ways where taking selfies might be a symptom of underlying problems in someone's life?*
- *When does taking selfies cross the line into something unhealthy?*
(www.trueactivist.com/scientists-link-selfies-to
-narcissism-addiction-mental-illness/)

This is an earth-shattering statement when you really think about it. Culture today has somehow decided that fashion and beauty are the same thing. So how can you become beautiful? With a spray tan, makeup, and a killer outfit, of course. By hitting the gym and hitting the mall. And most of us have just gone along with this message. We believe the most beautiful girls are the ones who are fit and fashionable, and we exalt them as our inspiration. Maybe not with our words, but definitely with our actions. Don't believe me? Just check your boards on Pinterest. The underlying message is that beauty can be bought.

When I read 1 Peter, I'm a little bit encouraged to know that girls who lived thousands of years ago struggled with the same image problems that I face today. Social media didn't create the "beauty can be bought" idea, it only made it more accessible. As girls, this need to feel beautiful is another one of those values that's buried deep in our souls. We won't escape the need, and we aren't supposed to. We just need to figure out a healthy way to get that need met. But the lies that swirl across every culture, every time period, and every heart can make the right answer hard to find.

I wish the women in Peter's church hadn't struggled with distorted ideas of beauty. I wish that we didn't struggle with it either. Because the idea that fashion equates to beauty is an absolute lie. And when we believe lies instead of the truth, it can wreck hearts and lead to some messy realities in our lives.

> *Some of these "messy realities" affect some of us girls in ways that run much deeper than selfies or spray tans. My sweet friends, if you are struggling with an eating disorder or self-harm, please turn to Appendix 1 before you read on. I have some special words waiting there just for you.*

•••

When we start believing that beauty is only about our bodies, we end up spending our time and money and energy chasing that kind of beauty. And as a girl who chased it for years, I know it's exhausting.

CHASING AN ILLUSION

Do you know what happens when you chase culture's version of beauty? You never catch it. You just keep running and running, hoping to finally reach that ideal definition of beauty. And maybe for a fleeting moment, you think you got it right. You feel on top of the world, admiring your fitness, your style, your skin tone. But how long does that feeling ever last? As soon as you hop on Instagram or Tumblr or Pinterest, there she is: someone "more perfect" than you. She's skinnier or more athletic or more put together. And suddenly, you're not good enough again. And so you have to start chasing the ideal all over again.

Do you ever wonder what Jesus thinks about all this? When we chase this crazy standard of beauty, we end up defeated and broken and worn out. Maybe some of you feel that way right now. I think that breaks His heart. Know why? Because God *did* design you and me to run hard after something. But that something is Him. When we chase Jesus, we end up being healed and refreshed. And *that's* what God wants for you—not the exhaustion and emptiness that comes from chasing beauty.

But in a world screaming that beauty can be bought, how do you step out of that race?

You have to stop chasing the wrong things before you can start chasing the right ones. And before your feet will stop running, your heart has to stop believing the lie.

Beauty can't be bought. And it's easier to see through that lie when we recognize that true beauty isn't physical.

#FACTCHAT

Over the ages, women have tried all kinds of crazy things to achieve beauty. In an effort to have dainty feet, the Chinese would break young girls' toes and bind their feet to prevent them from growing! Women in Elizabethan England would apply lead-based powder to their skin in order to achieve a pale complexion, despite the fact that it might cause baldness or skin inflammation. And in the sixth century, aristocratic women would try to

achieve this fair-skinned look with controlled bleedings —
literally draining the color out of their bodies!

- What are some of our beauty rituals today? Do you think
  future generations will think any of them seem crazy?
- Even women who are very beautiful by culture's standards have admitted to feeling insecure about their
  appearance. Why do you think this is?
- What's the difference between being attractive and being
  beautiful?

(http://mom.me/mind-body/7471-weirdest-beauty
-rituals-throughout-history/)

BEAUTY . . . OR DECORATION?

I recently moved into a new apartment. I spent weeks shopping for furniture and paint colors and picture frames and, most
importantly, a bed. Sleeping, being comfortable, and ridiculous
amounts of throw pillows all rank very high on my list of priorities. And if you came to spend the weekend with me in my apartment, I hope you'd think my room was cool. Chevron and mint
green abound. Now let's say you walk into my room and you see
my big fluffy comforter, my decorative pillows, and my cute fleece
blanket folded at the end, and you decide that it looks really in-
viting. So you go to sit down on it—and you fall right through to
the floor! Imagine that I just laughed and said, "Oh, yeah, beds
are actually pretty expensive so I just set up all my stuff on some
cardboard boxes instead of buying a mattress. It looks cute though,

right?" You'd probably think I was absolutely crazy, and you would be right. It doesn't matter how cute my decorations are *if there's no bed underneath them*. It doesn't take a genius to figure that out.

But isn't that exactly what we do with beauty?

Makeup and highlights and designer jeans are fun. There's nothing wrong with any of them. But they are *not* what make you beautiful, just like pillows and blankets are not what make a bed. The truth is you are already beautiful. Nothing you wear or mask or change can ever add to your beauty, and none of those things can take away from it, either. Will they make you more "attractive" to the world? Maybe. But attractiveness and beauty are not synonyms. Never have been. Never will be.

You can never buy your own beauty. Not through products or shopping sprees or gym memberships. Beauty doesn't rest on any of that.

BEAUTY AT A STEEP PRICE

Now what I'm about to say might seem contradictory at first. So stick with me. You can't buy your beauty because it's already been purchased. God, the One who created us and loves us fiercely, knows that we can't escape the lies. We don't even know that we're walking in the midst of them. We get stuck in sin, and we can't afford our own salvation. But because God cares about our hearts, He offers to buy our freedom for us. Freedom from the world's standards of beauty. And freedom from so much more. He offers freedom from all the sin that we've been so entangled in, from the certain death that we are facing if we're left on our own.

Can we hop down a rabbit trail for a minute? I want to dig into what this freedom really means. You might not think you are all that stuck. Maybe you're not even sure what "sin" is, exactly, or that it's something you need to be freed from. But as you've been reading these last few chapters, maybe your heart has understood the struggles I've been writing about. Do you wish you could be freed from them? The reason we all fight so hard to find acceptance and worth is because we don't have it. Something *is* inherently missing from our lives. When we're empty, we desperately grasp at things to fill the void. Social media is just one of the things we turn to, but it will never be the thing that finally satisfies. In fact, only one thing can.

Do you know what you're really craving?

A connection to God.

Value. Affirmation. Peace. All of those things come from being connected to God. The problem is that we're born separate from Him. Why? Because God is perfect in every way. And He can't be in the presence of imperfection. But we're all imperfect, aren't we? We mess up. We're mean. We tell lies and we believe them. We were created to connect with God, but we're too messed up to reach Him. Yet He still loves us. He wants to fill us up just as much as we desire to fill our empty places.

So what does He do? Something radical. Something incredible.

God sent His son, Jesus, to this earth. He sent Him to walk with humanity, to be like us, even though He's the one who *made* us. And if that's not wild enough for you, Jesus also died for us. He was perfect. And because He never sinned, His sacrifice bridged the gap between our sin and God's holiness. He couldn't be defeated by death, though. Jesus was raised to life three day later, and He's still alive and powerful and completely in love with you. Because of that one incredible act of love, we can be picked up out of our mess.

Now, maybe you're wondering what this all has to do with the idea of beauty and social media. The cross of Jesus is something you usually hear about in church, not something that shows up alongside selfies. Well, you know that ache we've been trying to dull? The emptiness we've been trying to fill with approval from selfies and Tweets? There's a way to fill that up. For good. Redemption opens the door for us to find all we need and more.

Grace is what makes us beautiful. Grace means getting something we don't deserve. And at the cross, God gave the biggest, most extravagant show of grace the universe has ever seen. Would God have bothered with all that if He didn't love you and cherish you and think you were already beautiful? We were bought with a price, the blood of Jesus. It's graphic and shocking. But it's also beautiful. God could punish us or ignore us. But instead He offers us saving grace. *And* the only thing we have to do is receive it and turn over our brokenness and emptiness to Him. Can you believe that the God of the universe would do something so crazy for messed-up people like you and me? Trust me, though. Your mess doesn't scare Him, and He knows just what to do with it.

Can you think of a person who may be unattractive by culture's standards but whom everyone loves because of the beauty he or she has inside? #GiveItATry

•••

Whether you've heard this story of grace a hundred times or you're laying eyes on it for the very first time, let me encourage you to start acting on it. Today. Right now. Just hearing and knowing something won't change your heart. But when you pray and believe, you begin the coolest journey of your entire life. I am living proof of it. Jesus didn't make all of my problems and struggles vanish, but He does walk beside me through them. Sin hasn't disappeared from my heart, but now I know how to fight it. Every broken piece I've surrendered to God has been lovingly placed back together. Friends, it has been *so* worth it. It's the most important decision I ever made. If this extravagant grace is what you need or if you'd like to read more about it, please flip to Appendix 2 in the back of this book. I'd love to talk with you about it there.

The moment we choose to accept this redemption on our behalf, we are covered with Christ's perfection. To God, you are worth the very highest price.

No amount of bronzer or number on a scale or Pinterest-worthy outfit could ever make you more valuable than you already are in the eyes of your Creator. First Corinthians 6:20 sums it up so well: "You have been bought and paid for, so honor God with your body." Does that mean shying away from fitness or fashion? Nope. But it does mean knowing that your beauty doesn't come from them. Decide right now not to let your body become your god. Choose Jesus—He's much better at it.

Don't try to make yourselves beautiful on the outside, with styl-ish hair or by wearing gold jewelry or fine clothes. Instead, make yourselves beautiful on the inside, in your hearts, with the endur-ing quality of a gentle, peaceful spirit. This type of beauty is very precious in God's eyes.

—1 Peter 3:3-4

IDENTITY: TAKING IT BACK

1. Are you using your body to make you feel valued or affirmed? If so, how? Are you dressing immodestly, obsessed with getting your hair and makeup perfect, or addicted to fitness and dieting? Our bodies are incredible creations of God, but they were never designed to get the glory. Decide today how you are going to fight the lie that your physical self determines your value.

2. What part of your inner beauty might be lacking? I know that I need to work on being gentle. I need to speak truth to my friends, but I need to make sure I'm doing it with kindness and love. What is Jesus telling you to change about your beauty that comes from within?

Chapter 5

PIN THIS, NEED THIS

When Materialism Fights for Our Hearts

My closet is filled with hundreds of fashionable outfits. Chevron, tribal print, and killer color combinations abound. I have a perfect pair of shoes for every occasion and, of course, the jewelry to match is hanging right alongside. Feeling jealous right about now?

Before you hate me and stop reading, I should probably tell you that this closet is imaginary. Well, to be fair, it's very real. But it only exists in the virtual world.

Yes, it's a board on Pinterest.

I titled it "Imaginary Closet."

Rest easy. The search for perfect outfits eludes me in real life just as often as it does you. The day I find a pair of white jeans that are both classy and slimming will be a day of great rejoicing, I assure you. But I'm not going to discuss my real-life closet conundrums—that's a whole different book. Today, I want to talk about my imaginary closet, and why it is that I need one.

PINTEREST DREAMING

I'm a self-proclaimed fashionista and a recovering shopaholic. I like clothes. And shoes. And jewelry. And more clothes. When Pinterest came into the spotlight, it was a happy day in my little world. What girl wouldn't love searching for inspiration and ideas when it comes to all things fashion—particularly when those ideas are free? In the days after I got my account, it was a sure bet that you'd find me with a latte in one hand and my mouse in the other, pinning furiously. I was having a great time.

Then I discovered all the other great categories.

The number of boards on my account grew from two to fifteen. I started planning décor for my future apartment and pinning recipes for all the meals I would cook in my cute little kitchen. I found quotes and DIY projects to accompany these events that were sure to take place, eventually. It was all very inspiring.

One day, though, something happened. I looked around my wonderfully decorated room, into my full closet and full refrigerator. And I felt kind of dissatisfied. It was subtle—discontentment always is—but I started to yearn for the world I'd created on Pinterest instead of the one I had right in front of me. I would stare at my clothes in the morning and think, "This would be the perfect time to wear that dress I pinned the other day." I looked at my bedroom and thought, "I'm tired of this color scheme. I wish I could just click the room I saw online into existence right here." These thoughts started off as occasional pricks in my mind but turned into daily discontentment with my belongings and my circumstances.

For a while, I didn't see the problem. After all, I wasn't setting my credit card on fire by actually purchasing any of these things. They were just ideas. Things I'd love to have some day down the road. Things that would make my life a little bit better.

Did you catch that last one? *Things* that would make my life a little bit better.

Really?

And there it was. An ugly lie that had slowly worked its way into my heart as I pinned to my heart's delight. I'd started to believe that what I already had was not enough. I needed one more outfit, one new meal, one new DIY project, and *then* my life would be picture-perfect.

The dictionary defines materialism as "a preoccupation with or stress upon material rather than intellectual or spiritual things." And discontentment is "a longing for something better than the present situation; not satisfied."

Ouch. Those definitions resonated with my heart in ways I hadn't noticed until Webster so bluntly pointed them out. So I decided to do a little Word-searching and see what Jesus had to say about my situation. Surely He would understand that I just wanted my outfits, meals, and home to be fashionable, right?

#FACTCHAT

According to a July 2014 research report, American teenagers have a total annual income of $91.1 billion. An impressive $258.7 billion dollars is spent on teenagers each year (Adding the items parents buy for their kids with those teenagers buy for themselves). When you spread that amount over the 26,873,000 teenagers in the USA, that's an average $9,626 being spent on each teenager every year.

- What are some of the most popular products that teen-agers and their parents spend money on? Do you think teens tend to be content with what they have?
- If you had exactly $9,626 to spend for a year, what would you spend it on? What would you splurge for? What would you be unable to afford? How much would you save or give to important causes?
- Can money buy happiness? Why or why not? (www.statisticbrain.com/teenage-consumer-spending-statistics/)

RICH KID LEARNS A LESSON

As it turns out, Jesus has a lot to say about material things. Scripture is chock-full of verses for us to hold in our hearts when materialism comes knocking on our doors. In fact, in Mark 10, Jesus had a conversation with a guy whose heart sounds a lot like mine. The basic story goes something like this. A wealthy young guy comes up to Jesus and wants to know how to get eternal life—he wants to follow Him. Jesus tells him to take all his things and sell them or give them to the poor, and then the guy will be freed up to follow Him anywhere. And in the end, since the guy had a lot of things and giving them up would make him sad, he turned

Jesus' offer down and walked away. (You can find the entire story in verses 17-31 if you'd like to check it out.)

So does that story mean you have to be broke and homeless before following Jesus? Not at all. I don't think becoming a penniless wanderer is an across-the-board requirement at any point during our walk with Him. But there's a lesson that the rich young guy needed to learn, and it's a point that still rings true for us today. What if Jesus *did* call you to give up material things? Would you willingly surrender your Pinterest-styled life, or would you walk away?

Do you ever feel like the things you have need just a little bit of work? Do you ever find yourself thinking life would be better with just one more thing? It's so easy to do. But is an upgraded closet, better cooking skills, or a better decorated room really going to provide the contentment your heart craves? In today's culture our hearts have been groomed to think so. My friend Kate recently described her feelings about the impact of Pinterest this way: "We think the life painted on our screens by millions of photos crammed together should be real life. Sometimes when I am picking out clothes or putting on makeup, my mind flashes to that nameless beauty on my screen. All of a sudden I want to copy and paste that to my face and body."

Copy and paste. That's what we really want, isn't it?

Instant gratification and immediate upgrades. And since there's no copy-and-paste feature in real life, we end up discontent with the world we live in.

#FACTCHAT

Eighty percent of Pinterest users are women. What are they pinning? The most popular categories are crafts, recipes, and quotes.
(www.digitalsherpa.com/blog/25-amazing -pinterest-facts/)

When I started recognizing this gnawing discontent in my own heart, I knew something needed to change. So I headed back to the story of Mark 10 and put myself in the shoes of our wealthy friend, asking myself what Jesus would say to *me*. It wasn't a fun scenario. I realized that the story wasn't really about selling my home or having zero dollars to my name. Jesus was challenging me to think about what was ruling my heart. If push came to shove, would I choose things over Jesus? Was I preoccupied with material things rather than spiritual ones?

I had to admit, there were moments when I answered those questions with a yes. In those moments, I was serving possessions rather than Jesus. And I don't know about you, but a full closet and a well-decorated home are nice enough, but they seem like terrible gods to me. So I set out to dethrone them.

Have you been in my shoes? Ever found yourself obsessed with the styles you were pinning, and discontent when your real life didn't match up? If you have, you are not alone. I'm daily fighting the desire to blaze right through the line between casual inspirations and consuming desires. You know what helps me out in this battle? Knowing that Jesus will never send me into it unequipped.

BATTLE STRATEGIES

Hebrews 13:5 challenges us to be free of the love of money and to be content with what we have instead. That's a tall order, don't you think? Thankfully, God doesn't just spit commands at us and walk away. He's okay with our questions, and His answer is not "Because I said so." For the answer to this materialism fight, check out the second part of the verse: "After all, [God] has said, *I will never leave you or abandon you*." Friends, we're called to let go of our material obsessions because the One who owns it all already walks with us, providing for our every need. In fact, Philippians 4:19 tells us just that.

Actually, if we were creating a Pinterest board filled with wisdom, I think the Apostle Paul, the author of Philippians, would be worth repinning. Paul is the guy in the Bible whose life I really am the *least* envious of. If you head over to 2 Corinthians 11, you can get the full activity log of his life, but I'll highlight some of the craziest events for you: prison, beatings, snake bites, shipwrecks, starvation, death threats.

Yeah, don't sign me up for that. None of that sounds like a good time, does it?

Even after suffering all that and more for the name of Jesus, this is what Paul says about materialism. "I know the experience of being in need and of having more than enough; I have learned the secret to being content in any and every circumstance, whether full or hungry or whether having plenty or being poor. I can endure all these things through the power of the one who gives me strength" (Philippians 4:12-13).

Did Paul really feel *content* with his crazy difficult life? As many times as I've read that verse, I'm still floored when I consider what he went through and his contentment against all odds.

And here I am whining that I don't have enough summer dresses. Anyone else feeling a little convicted? I really need to start wearing steel-toed boots whenever I study the Bible, because I get my toes stepped on every time.

But you want to know my favorite part of Paul's verse? There's a *secret*. Every girl loves to know a good secret. And Paul has a great one. If we want to be content in every circumstance—content with our current wardrobe, content with our current décor, content with the things we have *right now*—here's the secret to success: seek Jesus.

That's it?

It really is! The beautiful thing about walking with Jesus is that it's simple. So simple, in fact, that people often run around trying to add things to it. Maybe you've heard people adding rules like, "Thou shalt not have a Pinterest account, for it is a snare and a pitfall." But I don't remember reading that as commandment eleven, do you? The solution to our struggle with materialism isn't deleting our accounts or selling everything to Plato's Closet or never shopping again. The solution? We need to set our hearts and minds on Christ.

As it turns out, what most needed a makeover in my life wasn't my bedroom or my recipe book or my closet. It was my heart, my priority list, and my focus. Buying the latest and greatest satisfies us for a moment, or a few days at best. But finding "godliness" and "being happy with what you already have" is "a great source of profit" (1 Timothy 6:6).

How would you feel differently if you spent ten minutes typing a list of all your blessings versus ten minutes wishing for new things on Pinterest? #GiveItATry

• • •

Even though turning to Jesus is a simple concept, it can be hard to do in the glare of a Pinterest-crazy world. So while I'm definitely not advising you to run from these websites forever (my account is still up and running, and I get on it from time to time), I would encourage you to spend some time away if materialism is something you struggle with. Give yourself a little space to refocus your heart. Maybe you try something like this for a week: Every time your heart tugs at you to look for a new outfit or project to tackle, you head to the Bible for a few minutes instead. Or come up with another creative way to take a break from pinning and refocus your mind toward Jesus. Whatever you choose to do, I hope you'll discover the life, joy, and contentment that God's waiting to pour into your thoughts and heart.

Believe me, Pinterest pales in comparison. There's nothing like the thrill of running hard after Jesus.

Godliness is a great source of profit when it is combined with being happy with what you already have.
—1 Timothy 6:6

IDENTITY: TAKING IT BACK

1. What have you been wishing you could "copy and paste" into your own life? Why do you feel like you need that thing to be content?

2. Do the hard seasons of Paul's life make you uncomfortable? They sure make me feel thankful I haven't experienced all of that horrible stuff. His secret to contentment was simply to love Jesus: how can you chase after that same contentment in your life today?

WORDS, WORDS, WORDS

The power of words. It's not something we think about very often, especially when it comes to social media. But aren't words the whole point? We use social media to convey our words to the people who follow us online. And those words impact us.

Have you ever read a Tweet that made you laugh out loud? Or a Facebook update that made you feel angry? Words on social media have the power to encourage or discourage, bring laughter or tears. And in the same way the words you read affect you, the words that you type on a screen are affecting others. Those words are important: just as important as the ones that you speak with your tongue. They can change someone's mood or someone's day. Maybe even their life.

Words matter.

If you took nothing else from the last few chapters, I hope you heard this loud and clear: You matter. The God of the universe is crazy about you. He loves you more than you could ever even comprehend. And He says that you are more valuable than any social media statistic could ever show.

Words matter. Let's find out why.

Chapter 6

"A LITTLE BIRD TOLD ME"

How Words Get Tossed Around

I liked school a lot as a kid, and even if that labeled me as a nerd, I was proud of it. Learning was super fun, in my little opinion, and I loved getting report cards because I had worked hard and gotten a lot of good marks that I could show off and stick on the refrigerator with my Hello Kitty magnets. (More like hello, throwback. Is Hello Kitty even around anymore?) I was always really proud of those grades.

What I dreaded was the comments section—those horrible blank lines where my teachers could describe to my parents *in their own words* what I was up to during the day. I got the same comment. Every. Single. Time. For years. Want to guess what that comment was?

"Jessica is a great student, but she talks too much."

Well, at least I was consistent.

I really liked words. I liked writing them and speaking them often, even when other people were trying to do their work, which turned out to be a problem with my teachers. By second grade, it was obvious that words were going to be a big part of my life.

LOVE AFFAIR WITH WORDS

A decade and a half later, I still love words. Mostly because I like people, and talking to them is fun. But I also like words because they tell stories. Think about it. So much about who you are is locked up in memories and experiences and plans for the future, in feelings and ideas and lessons you've learned. The only way you get to share those things with people is to use words. You use them to paint pictures of places you've been, to weave stories about your life. And as people listen, they understand more than just the stories; they also start to understand you.

Words are one of the best gifts God gave us here on Earth. We may not think about that gift very often, but we should. We shouldn't take words for granted, because they matter to God. How do we know? Because He mentions it. Multiple times. In multiple books of the Bible.

In fact, let's peek into Genesis 11 as an example. It's a crazy story, and you should check it out in its entirety sometime. But here's the gist: the whole world spoke only one language at this point in history. God had commanded people to spread across the earth and populate it after the flood, but instead they just kept living on this one plane and hanging out with one another. And then, in addition to their disobedience, they got prideful. They decided that if they all worked together, they could build a tower high enough to reach God. For some reason I've never quite understood, they figured that a tall building would give them power and fame, and they could avoid having to spread out and obey God. Which is especially funny to me since the entire population of the world was participating. Who was going to think they were famous? Obviously, God wasn't okay with this prideful idea. He punished the people by confusing their languages so they couldn't communicate anymore.

I love the fact that God—the One who flooded the entire world and has endless power—chose to punish the people by giving them different languages to speak. It will never stop being awesome to me. This story shows me that God cares about words just as much as I do. Maybe even more.

And while it's a little bit humorous to think about waking up one day and hearing your next-door neighbor speaking German or Chinese when you'd only ever known this one common language, we need to take a serious look at the fact that this story proves beyond a shadow of a doubt that words matter. God will not stand for pride or disobedience in our words, because what we say leads to what we do. He will not sit idly by while we murmur against Him and throw careless ideas around. We're not even halfway through the first book in the Bible, and it's all too apparent that our Creator is passionate about words.

#FACTCHAT

Every second, on average, around 6,000 Tweets are sent on Twitter. That's over 350,000 Tweets sent per minute, 550 million per day, and around 200 billion Tweets per year!
(www.internetlivestats.com/twitter-statistics/)

THE WORD ON WORDS

But the interaction between this all-powerful God and our words doesn't stop in Genesis 11. Far from it. And when the God of the universe brings something up over and over in His word, I'm learning to pay attention to it.

I have to admit, when I started researching Bible verses about our words, I expected to find advice about actual words. What we should say, when and how we should say it, specific phrases to avoid, and things like that. I did find some of those verses, and we'll get to them. But I also found some other verses that really surprised me, because they were about *not* using words.

Proverbs is a book of the Bible that's filled to the brim with wisdom. The verses are easy to memorize, but sometimes really hard to live out. Especially when they're about words—and especially for a girl who loves to speak and write lots of words every single day. Yet even in the midst of my love affair with all things grammar, I can't deny the truth of Proverbs 17:27, which starts off saying, "Wise are those who restrain their talking." There's just no getting around it. If I want to be a wise girl, I have to hold back my words on occasion. Sometimes, they just don't need to be said, because they're not kind, true, or necessary.

Now maybe you're like me, and you're thinking, "Well, I don't feel all that wise sometimes." This proverb has that covered, too. Just read the next verse. "Fools who keep quiet are deemed wise; / those who shut their lips are smart." Well, there we have it. Right there in Scripture, it tells us how we can keep ourselves from foolishness. Sometimes all we have to do is just shut our mouths.

I won't try to make this idea super complicated, because it's not. Sometimes the wisest, kindest, and best decision you can make is to say nothing at all. It may be a simple idea, but I know that it's probably hard for some of you, because it's really hard for me. (Incessant talkers, unite.) But I also want to be wise, and I want to honor Jesus. And I hope you do, too. So let's keep trying.

If one verse isn't enough to convince you, though, buckle up and hang on. God's given us some more kickers to think about. Check out Proverbs 13:3, which simply says, "People who watch their mouths guard their lives." Now, I'm not telling you that your words, or lack thereof, will physically save you from danger. (Although it's possible, don't you think? My overactive imagination just thought of several scenarios where quietness could equal salvation.) What I do know is that careless words can make life messy. Like the time I walked up to one of my classmates in fourth grade and told her I was sorry she forgot it was picture day because if she'd known, she would have worn a prettier shirt. Yeah, I really said that. Honesty was my gift; tact was not.

Sadly, though, fourth grade was not the last time I was careless with my words. I'm wincing as I think about the many times I've thrown sentences out with no thought of how they would be taken. Proverbs 10:19 rings true in my heart: "With lots of words comes wrongdoing, but the wise restrain their lips." Notice how that wisdom thing keeps coming up? But what does wisdom with words even look like? And what does it have to do with social media?

KNOWLEDGE IS NOT WISDOM

In our desire to become wise women, it's important to note that knowledge and wisdom are *not* the same thing. Knowledge is based on facts; wisdom is based on obedience. You could write, memorize, and lecture about the damage that comes from slamming your hand in a car door. You could study the difference between nerve damage and tissue damage, outline the process and timeline of healing, and hand out a sheet of statistics about how many people fall prey to this common injury every year. You would probably have a lot of knowledge about the subject at that point. But you could still walk out to your car, throw your backpack into the back seat while you're focused on typing a text message, and slam your hand in the door. That would be unwise. Your friends would probably laugh at the irony—but hopefully they'd get you some ice.

That may sound like a ridiculous example, but do you see my point? We can spew facts all day long and still be none the wiser. Becoming wise women involves much more than memorization. It involves action. It's putting feet on your facts.

Knowledge means that I can quote those verses from Proverbs to you. Wisdom means that I actually start holding my tongue once in a while. Wisdom means weighing my words before I speak them, and choosing to say only things that are kind, true, and necessary. Wisdom recognizes that careless words don't add anything of value to the conversation.

I may have graduated beyond fourth-grade-picture-day rudeness, but I still let careless words fly at times. Only now, instead of speaking them with my tongue, I'm usually tapping them out with my thumbs. Social media is my venue of choice when it comes to unwise words these days. Could it be one of yours too? Some of you are probably thinking, *This isn't really for me—I'm not one of those mean girls online. I really do say kind stuff on my accounts.* High five for being kind online. That's awesome. (And If you *are* one of those self-proclaimed "mean girls," or if you've been the victim of one, especially when it comes to social media, we'll talk more about that later.) But I want to remind you all that kindness to others, while it's definitely something to strive for, doesn't always equal wisdom. Sometimes, the person who hurts most because of your careless words is yourself.

#FACTCHAT

In October 2014, Harris Interactive released a survey of 812 American teens and their perceptions about social media use. What did they find? Respondents indicated frustration with their friends for not "being themselves" on social media. Approximately 80 percent complained that people their age share too much on social media. And two thirds of respondents said they have stopped sharing as much information as they used to.

- What are some examples of over sharing that you've seen on social media sites?
- Why do you think some people over share? What are they trying to accomplish?

> • *How much is too much? In other words, what kind of things should be off limits for sharing on social media? (www.cnbc.com/id/102112733#)*

WORDS THAT WOUND

I'm a great secret keeper. I value loyalty in friendships more than almost anything else. So if you tell me something that I need to keep silent about, I'm a steel trap. There's only one exception: my own life. I've realized that there's a really big gap between wisdom with my friends' secrets and wisdom with my own.

Does anyone relate? I'm the world's best secret keeper with my friends' stories, but when something happens in my own life, I turn into a chronic over sharer. I tell everyone and I tell everything. This *is not* wise behavior. And that's a message I've had to preach to myself, over and over. On many occasions, I've created awkward situations for myself due to my big mouth. And sometimes, I'm sad to say, there has been irreparable damage to friendships that I really treasured because I just could not stop talking.

A few years ago, I got an opportunity to work with some kind of famous people on a really cool project. (The "who" and "what" are not necessary for this story, so I'm going to be wise here and not over share.) I talked about this opportunity, and I talked about it a lot. I was humbled that I even got to be a part of this project, and I was really excited, and I couldn't wait to get started and. . . . You get the picture, don't you? In hindsight I can see how my talking got old really fast. I was talking about the opportunity because I was truly excited, but it came across to some people as bragging. A few people even started questioning whether I thought I was better than them. *Of course I didn't!* But my over sharing of the whole process made them think so. It was just messy and not very wise.

You probably appreciate a good guy story, right? Well, for the sake of encouraging you to choose words wisely, I'll share my most cringe-worthy story of all: I liked a guy. And I told people about it. And told more people about it. And kept telling people about it—until it became common knowledge. Then, when things didn't work out, I had to go back to all those people and explain the whole thing again, just to save face. It was not a fun time. And to this day, I still get, "Hey, remember when you liked _____?" Yep. I sure do. Now I'd really like to stop talking about it.

Through those and countless other blunders, I've learned to get on my knees and pray Psalm 141:3 like my life depends on it. "Set a guard over my mouth, LORD; / keep close watch over the door that is my lips." I love words, and I also love sharing life. Those are good things. But left unchecked, that combination tends to get me into hot water. Thankfully, my Jesus is the author of all wisdom, and He can give it to me when I ask. He can give it to you, too. And if we're feeling extra bold, we can even pray one step further. Psalm 19:14 says,

> Let the words of my mouth
> and the meditations of my heart
> be pleasing to you,
> LORD, my rock and my redeemer.

Do your heart's musings honor God? I know, that's a really hard question. But your words and your heart are not disconnected. As Jesus points out in Luke 6:45: "The mouth speaks what the heart is full of" (NIV).

If you're careless with your words, chances are it's usually because you are careless with your heart.

Our hearts are the core of who we are. Our identities. That's what we've been fighting for with the turn of every page. And it's what social media will try to steal away from us, especially when it comes to tossing around unwise words. We can wage war on careless words by praying for deeply rooted wisdom in our hearts. Remember that God is fighting for our hearts, too—because He knows that words matter, both to us and to Him. He loves that we girls can speak 20,000 words every day. But He also loves us too much to let us sling them around, hurting others—and ourselves.

Dare to pray Psalm 19:14 over your life. Ask God to make the words of your mouth (including the ones you type) and the thoughts in your heart pleasing to Him. With your words, you can bring Him glory and speak life into the lives of countless people. That's the beauty of social media. You can use those thousands of words that you speak every day to declare truth and to share with hurting people that there's a holy God who loves them. He wants to set them free from the weight of careless words—and a million other things. Romans 10:15 says, "How beautiful are the feet of those who bring good news" (NIV). And it's true—the gospel being shared is always a beautiful thing. And we can share that truth without walking a single step, thanks to social media.

So be wise, friends, and be bold.

How beautiful are the thumbs of those who Tweet good news.

> *Let the words of my mouth*
> *and the meditations of my heart*
> *be pleasing to you,*
> LORD, *my rock and my redeemer.*
> —Psalm 19:14

IDENTITY: TAKING IT BACK

1. Which is harder for you, keeping other people's secrets or keeping your own? If you're guilty of chronic over sharing, maybe it's time to mend some relationships that have been broken because of your words. Is there anyone you need to apologize to for being careless?

2. It's always easier to stick to something when we're held accountable. Is there a friend you could ask to hold you accountable for using words that are kind, true, and necessary?

Chapter 7

SCREENSHOT

Moments Can Be Captured

High school can be full of dramatic days, but I remember one Tuesday afternoon that blew them all out of the water. In the middle of a history test, the dean of our school came in and asked all the tenth grade girls to go to a special assembly. I'm sure you can imagine the "ooh" sounds from everyone else in the class. Special assemblies never end well, do they? I had no idea what was going on, and I was always into a few shenanigans here and there, so there was cause for concern. But as we walked into the auditorium, it became clear that this had nothing to do with silly pranks. The three teachers standing silently on the stage indicated some serious business. It was like the gym scene straight out of *Mean Girls*, only it was happening right in front of me.

So what was all the drama about? In short, there were two girls who didn't like each other. At all. It was a well-known fact. And for whatever reason, the conflict had escalated outside of school hours and landed on the comments thread of someone's profile picture.

A lot of mean things were said by girl #1. A *lot*. She called girl #2 things that I can't write down in this book, tagging her in every comment so she would be inclined to read them. And then, after a few hours, she deleted the comments. She'd had her mean fun. And then gotten rid of the proof.

Or so she thought.

Girl #2 printed out those comments before they were deleted. She brought copies of them to school just so everyone would know how mean this other girl was. Girl #1 was shocked. She thought deleted meant gone. But she learned the hard way, that's not how it works. Moments can be captured.

The leadership of the school called the assembly to remind us how to be kind to one another online. And while I felt relieved that I wasn't at fault for anything, it was also an experience that made me realize that what we say and do online matters in a big way.

THE CRINGE EFFECT

If you're anything like me, sometimes you're scrolling through social media and you stumble on a Facebook status or a picture that makes you cringe. I'm pretty sure I've said, "Oh, social media is *not* the place for that," out loud, on multiple occasions. And I'm just talking about the last few weeks! Practically speaking, there are some things that we just shouldn't put on social media.

The Bible agrees.

Wait, you might be thinking. *The Bible? I don't remember reading anything in there about a string of mean Facebook comments.*

Well, the Bible has more to say about Facebook than you might think, as it turns out.

Of course, social media was thousands of years from existing when the Bible was written. But don't you think girls of every era have needed practical advice about what to say and do? The girls of Bible times didn't have screens to share on, but I'll bet they still had moments when their words blew up into drama.

Sometimes life just needs a strong dose of practical advice, doesn't it? Common sense kind of stuff. We get off track so fast sometimes, and in those moments, we need to hear wisdom that applies to where we are, *right now*. Thankfully, the Bible has that kind of practical advice. It gives us great guidelines to fight against foolishness.

Foolishness. What comes to your mind when you hear that word? To be honest, it makes me feel like I'm either a grandmother or a displaced time traveler from the days of Shakespeare. We could substitute *dumb*, but that sounds way too harsh. And *silly* just takes me back to my preschool days. So let's think about foolishness as being *unwise*. In particular, let's talk about being unwise on social media, and the ways we can avoid the cringe effect in our own lives.

#FACTCHAT

A recent survey conducted by CareerBuilder.com found that 40 percent of companies go on social media sites to research job candidates. Among the things that would make them disqualify a candidate: 50 percent nixed applicants who'd posted provocative photos, 48 percent were turned off by posts about drinking or drug use, and 24 percent said they've discarded job candidates after finding information that showed they had lied about their qualifications.

- *Besides future employers, can you think of other situations where someone could experience embarrassment or negative consequences for things they've posted on social media?*
- *In general, do you think people are willing to post more risqué content than they would be comfortable sharing in real life? Why or why not?*
- *Have you ever posted something that you later regretted and decided to delete?*

(www.computerworld.com/article/2498356/it-careers /what-facebook-posts-will-keep-you-from-getting-hired.html)

DELETED FOREVER OR FOREVER WISHING IT HAD BEEN DELETED?

Social media lets us share life with people we care about in real time. But there are some things we shouldn't share on the World Wide Web. Why? For starters, because it's permanent.

I realize there's a delete button for everything we could ever post. And Snapchats were created to disappear on their own so you wouldn't even have to worry about that extra "delete" step. But the truth is "deleted" doesn't really mean gone. Just like you can't "un-say" words once they've rolled off your tongue, you can't "un-Tweet" words or "un-send" pictures. They're out there. They've been seen by people, and maybe even saved to those people's phones. Remember girl #1 from my high school assembly? I don't want any of you to learn this lesson the hard way like she did. Sometimes those words and images become permanent, even though you'd like to make them disappear.

God's Word weighs in on this, too.

Here's what Ephesians 5:15-16 says about the way we live day in and day out: "So be careful to live your life wisely, not foolishly. Take advantage of every opportunity because these are evil times." Basically, this verse tells us we have a choice. As we walk through life, we can choose to be wise or unwise. That includes the times that I slide my cell phone out of my back pocket and check my social media accounts.

Before we go any further, I want to point something out. Did you notice that these instructions from God are about day-to-day life? If He gives us advice about our daily lives, then He must care about them. That's a simple concept. But it blows my mind to think about it.

This God who thought up everything from sunsets to snails, who designed the Sahara and sneezes, He cares about each one of us. There's nothing too big for Him to handle, and there's no detail too small for Him to care about. He's intimately acquainted with every one of your thoughts and with every moment of your existence. He loves you so much that He cares about every piece of who you are. And social media has claimed a pretty big part of us, hasn't it? Sometimes, my most repetitive action is hitting the refresh button on my news feeds. We shouldn't really be surprised that God has advice about handling social media.

Of course, some people think God just hands out a lot of rules. You know what I'm talking about, right? We all have them somewhere in our lives—those random rules that don't really make sense—and they're annoying. It's called *legalism*, and I'll save you the boring definition. Basically, legalism means inventing rules for the sake of having rules. They're not necessary. Sometimes they're not even important. But some people really like to make them up. Even in the days when Jesus was on earth, there were a group of religious leaders who made up a bunch of rules to "add" to the ones God had given. Some of these rules said things like, "you can only take so many steps on Sunday or it's not a day of rest" and "you're not allowed to eat fruit from trees you planted until three years have gone by." Sounds a little crazy, right?

Even though some of the rules *people* make might be rooted in legalism, your heavenly Father's rules will *always* be rooted in love. I promise. His heart is to protect you, to free you from sin and selfishness. He wants you to actually enjoy life as you walk with Him. He's not overprotective. He's not a killjoy. And He's not random. The instructions we find in the pages of Scripture always exist for our good. Even when we can't understand the specific reasons behind the rules, we can always trust they come from God's heart for us. When we follow His rules, we end up with good moments—not the kind we wish we could delete forever.

> **#FACTCHAT**
> *Speaking of random laws, in Iowa, it's a misdemeanor if you try to pass off margarine as real butter. In Massachusetts, you can be fined for dancing to the national anthem. And in New York, it's unlawful for three or more people wearing masks to gather in public.*
> *(www.businessinsider.com/most-ridiculous-law-in-every -state-2014-2)*

WISDOM RULES

So what are some of God's guidelines when it comes to choosing wisdom in our everyday lives? Well, take a look at how the Apostle Paul starts the Ephesians passage we read earlier. He prefaces it with a warning. "Be *careful* to live your life wisely" (5:15, emphasis added). I guess that means the walk of life must be tricky sometimes, then. When it comes to walking wisely through social media, I like the advice of James 3:17. It says, "Wisdom that comes from heaven is first of all pure; then peace-loving, considerate, submissive, full of mercy and good fruit, impartial and sincere" (NIV). James is pretty good at giving exhaustive definitions, and this is one of them. So let's unpack it piece by piece.

First of all, wisdom is pure. There are a lot of important characteristics packed into that verse, but James mentions purity *first*. We can't skip over this one, even though it might not be a conversation we all love. If Jesus thinks it's important, shouldn't we value it, too? Exercising purity on social media can take on a lot of different forms. Before we even consider what we post, let's talk about what we're looking at.

I'm sure you already know that Snapchat is sometimes used to send inappropriate pictures to people. And that you can find pictures and videos that should *never* see the light of day on pretty much any website, including Pinterest and Tumblr. It's important to be aware of these temptations to impurity, so that we can flee from them immediately. And I know that these issues aren't restricted to boys. Girls, the things we look at online can lead us to impurity, too. Lust affects us all, because we're all sinners.

So whatever it is that you enjoy looking at online, keep this question at the forefront: is it pure? Leave no doubt about it. And if there's ever any question in your mind about what you're choosing, run it through the filter of Philippians 4:8. "Whatever is true, whatever is noble, whatever is right, whatever is pure, whatever is lovely, whatever is admirable—if anything is excellent or praiseworthy—think about such things" (NIV). If the thing you're seeing, reading, or listening to doesn't line up with one of those ideas, that's a red flag. It's time to exit out. Immediately. It's not worth it.

In addition to guarding what we look at, we also have to guard what we send out for others to see. You know what I use Snapchat for? Sending really ugly faces I make to my best friends and pictures of my food. I should just call it Snackchat, honestly. But I realize that this app can be used for very different purposes. Sending risqué selfies might be a tempting way to get the right person's attention. But what happens when someone grabs a screenshot of those images that were supposed to just disappear? You'll probably be wishing it *was* just a picture of your snacks, not one of you in less-than-enough clothing.

But screenshots aren't the ultimate problem here. Unwise uses of social media are just symptoms of believing the same lie we keep fighting over and over: the lie that says you aren't already loved and valued just as you are. Soak your heart in this truth yet again: God loves you, and He's already defined you as beautiful. You don't need to Snapchat for affirmation. God's already given it to you.

The truth is, if a guy is willing to compromise his own purity by looking at those pictures, from you or anyone else, *then he's not the guy for you.* You're valuable and beautiful, and you deserve to be treated as such. When you're following Christ, your Father is the king of the whole universe. That makes you a princess, so live like one. Guard your purity. Demand respect. You're worth it.

How would you view yourself differently if you took a minute every day to search online for a Bible verse about God's love? #GiveItATry

•••

FROM FAIRY TALE TO SINNER STORY

I speak from experience when I say that chasing affection in the wrong ways will leave you bruised and broken. But when you rest in Jesus' love, He heals that brokenness and satisfies your heart far more than social media ever could.

Maybe, like me, you've tried to find approval in the wrong places. I played the comparison game for a long time, and I played it often. And even though none of the messier moments were captured on a screen, they were certainly captured in my heart for a long time. Our stories probably don't look exactly alike, but here's the cool thing about grace: it can impact each of our lives right where we are. We can all grow to look more like Jesus without losing our unique story.

I found Jesus in the middle of a story about dwarves and poisoned fruit. It may sound crazy now, but Snow White seems vividly real to a four-year-old girl. My mom and I had just wrapped up our reading time, and for some reason, my little mind had wandered to deeper places. "Mommy?" I asked, "Did the wicked stepmother go to heaven when she died?" My mom shook her head and said, "Probably not, sweetheart." I stared back, contemplating for a moment before responding. Finally, I piped up. "Well, when I die, I want to go to heaven with Jesus, not to hell with the wicked stepmother." And just like that, I prayed to accept Jesus into my heart. It's one of my first memories, and even now I can remember the joy of that night. I didn't know it all, but I knew that Jesus loved me and that I loved Him. And I wanted to spend forever in heaven by His side. My childhood was full of innocence and excitement and a sincere love for my Jesus.

I wish I could say it stayed that way forever. My heart started off in the right place, but I got distracted. As I grew up and started high school, the world started to whisper lies into my soul, and I started to believe. My dreams for life became less about serving Jesus and more about becoming the best. I wanted the credit, the recognition, and the reward. I started to play the comparison game, and I was determined to win. Pride was in every corner of my heart, and I didn't even realize it.

I also got into a relationship. And I brought all my pride with me. Somehow, I forgot what I had learned as a four-year-old, that I was already beautiful, already loved, and already valued. That truth faded into the background. In its place, I worked really hard to present my relationship as "perfect" on the outside. I wanted to be part of a power couple. I wanted other people to admire me. And it worked.

From the outside, it appeared that I had everything I ever wanted.

What people didn't know is that on the inside, everything was falling apart. I was constantly worrying about my "five-year plan," afraid that I might not accomplish all the dreams that I hoped to find value in. I was so caught up in making my relationship look good on the outside that I left no room for Jesus on the inside. I found myself compromising all the standards I'd set for myself all those years ago. Emotionally, physically, and spiritually, I made decisions that edged Jesus out of my relationship, my future, and my heart. And I justified it all by comparing my choices to girls who were "worse." I'd become a captive to all the lies I told everyone, including myself. And I couldn't even see it.

Thankfully, in the middle of my mess, grace walked in. When I was running the fastest away from Jesus, He came after me. One night during my freshman year of college, I woke up at 2:30 in the morning and suddenly saw the mess that sin had brought into my life. It was clarity I didn't even ask for, nothing short of divine intervention. In that moment, the burdens I'd been carrying because of my sin became clear, and I decided right then to let go of them, even if that meant also letting go of my relationship, my dreams, my career plans. On my dorm room floor, God broke my heart for what breaks His, even though I wasn't searching for Him at all. His relentless pursuit is woven into every step of my story. And He wouldn't stop until my heart was completely His.

That day, I started running toward God's love again instead of trying to escape it. And I've never looked back. Of course, some of the chains in my life took longer than a day to break. But I chose freedom, and I'm still choosing it every day.

Jesus lovingly taught me how to listen to His voice instead of all the lies the world screams. And as I listen, I can remember who I really am, who I've really been all along. Because of grace, God never stops viewing me as His holy, pure, blameless daughter. And the more I soak in that truth, the more I believe those things about myself, even though I've made lots of mistakes. Romans 8:1 is one of the most beautiful statements I've ever read: "There is now *no* condemnation for those who are in Christ Jesus" (NIV). I'm not condemned; I'm free.

And you can be, too.

One of the things I'm most passionate about in life is for you to know that you're free. Not just to think about it, but to *know* it. To walk in that freedom. Trust me, I know what it's like to have your identity stolen by the ways of the world. You'll hear whispers that you aren't loved. That you're not pure. Not worthy. Not beautiful. Not enough. But they are all lies. And I will wage war on those lies for as long as I have breath. I will tell even the messiest parts of my story if Jesus can use it to show other people the way to freedom. He knows every bit of the mess, and He still loves me.

That can be your story, too. In fact, it already is. God sees your mess, and He loves you anyway. Believing it will change everything.

CAPTURE THE GOOD STUFF

We've covered a lot of ground for a chapter that's about misuse of social media, but before we wind up this conversation, let's take a final look at those words from James 3:17: "Wisdom that comes from heaven is first of all pure; then peace-loving, considerate, submissive, full of mercy and good fruit, impartial and sincere" (NIV). There's a ton of great advice in those words that can help you cultivate wise moments online.

Let's zone in on *peace-loving* first. Another little phrase with huge implications. I'm sure you've seen your fair share of social media drama. For some reason, if you give us girls two thumbs and a screen, the claws come out in a whole new way. If you think this is just a teenage problem, think again. Last week my whole Facebook feed was full of two moms arguing over the fact that they invited each other to too many Mary Kay parties.

I'm not kidding.

What in the world is going on?

*What happens more in social media comment sections,
healthy debates or ugly word wars?
#WhatDoYouThink?*

•••

I don't think anyone is a big fan of conflict, but sometimes things happen and they need to be dealt with. That's OK. But we need to find a healthy place to work through it. *Social media is not that place.* Being peace-loving doesn't mean we have to run away from every conflict. In fact, avoiding problems is just as sinful as handling them with anger and drama. Being peace-loving means that we work through conflicts so that we can mend hurt and re-establish peace. When we love peace, that will always be our end goal. Do you think subtweeting about someone and blowing the whole thing up on social media sounds like a good peace plan? I doubt it.

Being peaceful means calling the person on the phone to solve the problem rather than airing everything in public. It means holding back from the sarcastic comment on someone's status, no matter how much you disagree. It means choosing not to become the referee in someone else's social media battle, because more people usually just means more problems. A good standard to keep in mind would be Psalm 34:14: "Seek peace and go after it!"

The next two words James encourages us to pursue go hand in hand: considerate and submissive. Being considerate means that you're willing to look out for others. Submission is being willing to put others above yourself, to let your preferences and rights and ideas take second place. They aren't exactly the same thing, but you know what? Consideration and submission produce the same result. They help you build a life that's more about others than it is about you.

There are countless ways to apply this to social media. Is one of your friends hurting, having a hard week, hating life right now? Look out for that. And when you see it, love that person. Social media is often a place where we go to be heard. We share our pictures and send our thoughts. But let's be girls who are willing to turn that equation on its head. Let's use social media to listen and love and serve other people. It'll shock the world. It might even shock them so much that they ask why. And getting to share Jesus is the best part of all.

At the end of the verse, James leaves us with this: "full of mercy and good fruit, impartial and sincere." He's calling us to go all-out with our love. We shouldn't encourage others on social media only once in a while. We should be *full* of encouragement. We should be known for it. And we aren't called to serve just our closest friends. Our love comes from Jesus, and He loves every single person with that reckless kind of love. Even that annoying user who posts selfies all the time. Or the one who's always throwing out opinions you don't agree with. James challenges us to love them all, on social media and face to face.

Moments can be captured. So make yours worth capturing. Rather than regretting and deleting the things that you say, make moments that point people to Jesus. Moments that cause people to realize that you're not like everyone else. Because you're not letting social media define who you are. You're believing what God says about you—and that makes all the difference.

> *Wisdom that comes from heaven is first of all pure; then peace-loving, considerate, submissive, full of mercy and good fruit, impartial and sincere.*
> —James 3:17 (NIV)

IDENTITY: TAKING IT BACK

1. What's the hardest part of choosing wisdom? I struggle sometimes to be full of mercy and kindness. I would rather just say three nice things a day and be done with it. But my heart is in the completely wrong place when I think like that. I should be filled with wisdom because I am seeking God. So what is the one area of wisdom you need to ask Jesus for?

2. Find a system that helps you think before you speak—or post. Maybe your background could be a Bible verse that reminds you that your words matter. Maybe when you type a Tweet, you could save it to your drafts for five minutes, and then read it again before you share it. There's no one way to practice wisdom. Brainstorm what could work for you.

Chapter 8

MISERY LOVES COMPANY

When We Feed Our Feelings

I can be a little dramatic sometimes. Running late to a meeting could potentially send me into a frenzy. I throw out statements like, "This person will probably hate me forever if I don't show up soon. This day is the *worst*." I've also been known to sit on the floor and cry because I'm too afraid of stinkbugs to kill them. I know. But I'm theatrical about good things, too. I throw killer surprise birthday parties. I love to celebrate, I love to plan, and I love to have people over. It's really the trifecta of fun. I also tend to live Tweet fun events like road trips or concerts. Which could be either obnoxious or hilarious, depending on your perspective. God bless the people who do life with me every day. Sometimes I'm just a lot of—everything.

I'm telling you about my daily theatrics so you'll know that I don't do things halfway, even when it comes to emotions. As a self-proclaimed "creative type," I understand that emotions are powerful. And I think about them a lot when I write. After all, I can write about truth all day long, but if I don't understand how you feel, I can't convey it in a way that will matter. We were created for connection. And I'm all about it.

When it comes to valuing emotion, Lysa TerKeurst may have said it best in her latest book, *Unglued*: "God gave us emotions. Emotions allow us to feel as we experience life. Because we feel, we connect. Our emotions are what enable us to drink deeply from love and treasure it. And yes, we also experience difficult emotions such as sadness, fear, shame, and anger. But I must remember God gave me emotions so I could experience life, not destroy it."*

She nailed it, didn't she? Our emotions help us connect, feel, and experience life in the fullest of ways. But as girls who've been defined by Jesus, we need to be careful. Emotions can be so strong in the moment, and it's all too easy to let them define us temporarily and lead us toward bad choices.

#FACTCHAT

Are teenagers more stressed out than adults? The answer is yes according to a 2013 survey by the American Psychological Association, which found teenagers reporting higher average stress levels than those reported by adults. Among the study's other interesting discoveries: Eighty-three percent of teens mentioned school as a stress trigger, and just under 60 percent said they experience

---

*Lysa TerKeurst, *Unglued: Making Wise Choices in the Midst of Raw Emotions* (Grand Rapids: Zondervan, 2012), 16.

stress because of having to manage too many activities. Forty percent reported feeling angry or irritable in the past month, 36 percent reported feeling nervous or anxious, and just over a third reported "having laid awake at night" because of stress.

- On a scale of 1 to 10, how stressed out do you feel most days? What factors cause stress in your life and the lives of people around you?
- How does social media affect stress: Does it contribute to stress or help take it away?
- What are some of the *unhealthy* ways people try to manage stressful or negative feelings? What are some *healthy* ways to them?

(www.washingtonpost.com/national/health-science /stressed-out-teens-with-school-a-main-cause/2014/02/14 /d3b8ab56-9425-11e3-84e1-27626c5ef5fb_story.html)

EMOTIONS—THE CAPTAIN OF YOUR HEART?

Think of the different aspects of yourself as members of a team. The spiritual, emotional, and mental pieces of you all work together to create your unique and beautiful heart. Emotions are a very necessary part of that team. But they make terrible captains. They lead us in a million directions at once, and many of those directions aren't wise ones. For example, emotions might lead you to lie down on the couch and eat an entire pint of ice cream after a hard day. Anyone else been there?

When I feel my emotions take the lead, I'm often tempted to just sit back and let them. But that almost never has positive effects in my life. When I allow my giddiness over good news to control me, I get absolutely nothing accomplished for days. I'll also send my friends to the point of no return with my hyperactivity. Sound familiar to you? It just feels natural to flip out when you make a sports team or get that text from a cute guy. As tempting as it is to get carried away with good emotions, it's the negative ones that can really get my heart off track. When I let anger control my decisions, someone ends up on the receiving end of a piece of my mind. And it's not pretty. When sadness or disappointment wins out over the truth, I end up with that Ben and Jerry's ice cream on the couch for far too long.

I wish we never had to experience negative emotions. But we all do sometimes, don't we? And here's what I've noticed: all too often, we girls let the fire of our emotions burn without any attempts to put it out. In fact, we feed it instead. And that's when the emotions can really end up burning your life.

Take sadness, for example. Have you ever noticed how easy it is to feed that emotion? Watching chick flicks after a breakup is going to make a girl cry, every time. She'll probably start to say things like, "I'm never going to find real love," and "That's just a script. All boys stink in real life!" Those are emotion-driven statements. You've probably heard them from your friends—or maybe your own mouth. But they're also lies. And while we hear many lies from the whispers of others, feeding our emotions in an unhealthy way is like speaking lies to ourselves. Misery loves company, and we tend to heap one lie on top of another until we're absolutely miserable.

> **#FACTCHAT**
> Emoji *has officially worked its way into the English language. It was added to the Oxford Dictionary in August 2013, along with other social media terms such as* tweep, facepalm, *and* srsly. *Yes, Srsly!*

PINTEREST PITY AND TEARFUL TUMBLRS

Chick flicks aren't the only "feeder" of feelings, though. Social media has made its own contribution to our emotional crises. Have you ever hopped on Pinterest or Tumblr to find other people who resonate with your feelings of sadness, hurt, or disappointment? Or maybe you've posted a frustrated status update hoping you'll get dozens of comments that join you in the rant? Let's be clear: walking through hard times with other people is *not* wrong. But walking through hard times with people who feed your emotions instead of feeding you truth? That's not healthy. Or wise.

Sometimes, social media sites turn into a gathering of people who are sharing life's misery. But do you think depressing quotes and sad songs and other miserable people are going to make anyone feel better? To get past misery, you need truth, not more misery. Getting on Tumblr every time you're upset can actually become a way to avoid truth rather than finding it. I'm not saying you should delete Tumblr and Pinterest and never look for a quote that

115

describes how you feel. But what's your motivation when you hop on those sites? If you're just looking for company for your misery, you should stop. It's only going to make you more miserable.

I'm *not* saying you shouldn't ever feel sad. Or hurt. Or giddy, for that matter. God gave us the ability to feel emotions, good and bad alike. We just need to understand that truth isn't dependent on how we feel. Remember the scene from *Finding Nemo* when Marlin and Dory encounter the anglerfish on the ocean floor? The fish entices them with her glow, but then ends up trying to turn them into a meal. Emotions can be just as deceiving and lead us to make foolish mistakes: they can't be the light we follow or they'll eventually swallow us whole. You know what makes for a healthier way of handling emotions? Soaking your hearts in the truth of God's word. It can show you the wise step to take, even in your most emotional moments.

LESSONS FROM A SENSITIVE GUY

King David was an emotional guy. Even though he was the king of Israel, he made a lot of big mistakes, like adultery and murder. Pretty big stuff, right? What's interesting is that even after all that, God called David "a man after His own heart." God loves messed-up people, even when emotions get the best of them—that's one of my favorite things about Him. But He also doesn't leave them in the mess. He helps them learn and grow from those mistakes.

If you read the stories about David sometime, you'll see that many of his poor life choices came because he let his emotions, rather than truth, lead his choices. Thankfully, David learned from those lessons. He learned the hard way, but he learned. And you know what? God never pushed David to be less emotional. Those of us who feel deeply don't have to change who God created us to be. But David did learn *where to take* his feelings. And where did he learn to go? Straight to the source of truth. To God Himself.

Half of the book of Psalms is attributed to David. When I read it, I sometimes feel like I'm peeking into someone's private journal. David's psalms are his prayers, and he poured out his heart to God on both the best days and the worst ones. Do you ever struggle with overwhelming emotions, like David did? Let's take a look at some of David's psalms and see how he handled them.

How do you think it would feel to pour out your feelings in a letter to God next time you're feeling overwhelmed? #GiveItATry

• • •

In Psalm 8, David is impressed by God. He's in awe of creation, rejoicing in God's power, and humbled that this holy God would love a sinner like him. Take a look:

> Lord, *our Lord, how majestic*
> *is your name throughout the earth!*
> *You made your glory higher than heaven!*
> *From the mouths of nursing babies*
> *you have laid a strong foundation*
> *because of your foes,*
> *in order to stop vengeful enemies.*

When I look up at your skies,
  at what your fingers made—
  the moon and the stars
  that you set firmly in place—
    what are human beings
      that you think about them;
    what are human beings
      that you pay attention to them?
You've made them only slightly less than divine,
  Crowning them with glory and grandeur.
You've let them rule over your handiwork,
  Putting everything under their feet—
    All sheep and all cattle,
    The wild animals too,
    The birds in the sky,
    The fish of the ocean,
    Everything that travels the pathways of the sea.
Lord, our Lord, how majestic is your name through-
out the earth!

Contrast those awe-filled words with Psalm 51:1-12, when David is deeply mourning his own sin.

Have mercy on me, God, according to your faithful
love!
  Wipe away my wrongdoings according to your great
  compassion!

Wash me completely clean of my guilt;
  purify me from my sin!
Because I know my wrongdoings,
  my sin is always right in front of me.
I've sinned against you—you alone.
  I've committed evil in your sight.
That's why you are justified when you render your
verdict,
  completely correct when you issue your judgment.
Yes, I was born in guilt, in sin,
  from the moment my mother conceived me.
And yes, you want truth in the most hidden places;
  you teach me wisdom in the most secret space.
Purify me with hyssop and I will be clean;
  wash me and I will be whiter than snow.
Let me hear joy and celebration again;
  let the bones you crushed rejoice once more.
Hide your face from my sins;
  wipe away all my guilty deeds!
Create a clean heart for me, God;
  put a new, faithful spirit deep inside me!
Please don't throw me out of your presence;
  please don't take your holy spirit away from me.
Return the joy of your salvation to me
  and sustain me with a willing spirit.

David wasn't afraid to express emotions, good or bad, to the God who created him. You don't have to be afraid, either. There's no emotion too deep, no mess too big, and no problem too complicated for God to handle. David's story shows us that even adultery and murder were not too much for God to cover with grace. He knows about your messes already. And He'd love to walk through every step of them with you. Will you let Him?

GOOD COMPANY FOR A BROKEN HEART

Broken hearts, broken dreams, and broken promises all matter to God. You don't have to hide your pain. But don't wallow in it, either. Instead, hand it over to the God whose hands are big enough to hold it. Be honest with Jesus about the way you feel. I think you'll find out that He understands you the best and loves you the most—far more than anyone who might comment on your social media sites. Misery might love company, but you know what your heart really longs for? The presence of Jesus. He's the best company of all.

Let's learn to rejoice in our emotions. On the best days and the worst days, we can embrace emotions rather than burying them. After all, they're an important part of experiencing life, especially for us girls. But remember that emotions don't always reflect the truth. Whether you're walking through life's highs or lows, remember that Jesus has the last word about who you are—not the people or circumstances who might be making you feel unworthy or unloved. Doesn't that give your heart a boost of confidence? You can take everything you feel, big or little, to God because He understands every corner of your heart.

I'm even learning to pray for the emotional confidence to kill those terrifying stinkbugs. When I succeed, I'll Tweet about it so you guys know.

Maybe I'll even throw a party.

> *Your word is a lamp before my feet*
> *and a light for my journey.*
> —Psalm 119:105

IDENTITY: TAKING IT BACK

1. When emotions become really strong, what's your go-to place to air them out? Is it friends? Social media? A blog? Does that place point you to truth or does it allow you to sink deeper into your feelings?

2. Have you ever tried telling God about how you feel on the bad days? Sometimes, we thank Him when things are good but forget that He's just as capable of handling the bad. Next time sadness strikes, flip to the book of Psalms. You'll probably find one that covers how you feel. Try praying the words of that psalm out loud to God. He hears your heart when it's in pain, but sometimes we don't feel His love until we run to Him.

Chapter 9

"OOPS, WRONG PERSON"

When Words Cut Through a Screen

Have you heard the expression "sticks and stones may break my bones but words can never hurt me"? Whoever said that was lying. Words can hurt, and that's an understatement. Words can crush your spirit, kill your good mood, and even cause you to doubt truth. Proverbs 12:18 says that reckless words pierce like a sword. Have you ever felt that kind of painful power of words spoken to you? I know I have. I've felt deeply how painful they can be.

In fact, I'm feeling the effects of painful words right now. And when I say "right now," I mean it. Last night, words caused my heart to ache in a big way. I've been walking through a difficult few weeks with one of my most cherished friends. We share dreams over coffee, encourage one another to chase those dreams, and support one another when they seem out of reach. But all the world's chatter has been whispering lies in this friend's ear. And apparently those lies started to sound a lot like truth. I'll make a long story short: little doubts turned into big lies in my friend's heart. Which in turn caused this friend to lie to me in a big way—in a text message. Ouch! When I found out, it hurt my heart a lot.

I'm sure you've encountered drama of your own once or twice. As girls, it tends to pop up more than we care to admit. Being lied to is one of my least favorite things. Sometimes I think I'd prefer an actual slap to the face than to hear words that feel like a punch to the stomach. You know the feeling—all your organs just kind of drop and get tangled up and you feel like you can't breathe any more. That's how I felt when my friend lied to me.

But maybe there's an upside to this. Because in the middle of this really close friend delivering such hurtful words, I had to laugh a little and say, "Wow, Jesus, I guess writing about the pain words can cause will be extra genuine today."

Getting lied to hurts. But I'm learning to show grace. I'm learning to forgive. And I'm also learning that words have power, so I'd better be careful with mine. Proverbs 18:21 says, "Death and life are in the power of the tongue." That's a huge statement, isn't it? Let's not take it lightly. You and I know that words make a difference in our own hearts. We've felt the freedom of hearing loving words and realizing someone is on our side. But we've all been hurt, too. We've heard words that tore us down and minimized our worth, beauty, and value.

It's amazing how words can change everything like that.

WORDS = BFF BUILDING BLOCKS

As girls, we experience emotions in a very powerful way. Emotions shape who we are, how we feel, and how we relate to people.

Feelings are more foundational to us than they are to guys. Don't believe me? Just think about this: Have you noticed how guys become friends? It's usually through doing activities—sports, video games, or even yard work. But girls become friends through conversations. We go out to dinner, to coffee, or shopping—but we talk through it all. Relating to someone emotionally is how we grow closer to them. And words convey emotion. That's why we feel the pain of reckless words so deeply.

Words can make us feel so connected and close. But there's also a frustrating pattern I see when it comes to using words: I can be deeply hurt by words, but I sometimes use my own words to inflict pain in the hearts of people I love. I've been careless with what comes out of my mouth. I haven't quite perfected making the "words of my mouth and meditations of my heart" pleasing to God (Psalm 19:14). And truthfully, sometimes it's a lot worse than simple carelessness. Sometimes, I know that words are going to hurt, and I say them anyway. I'm guessing most of you have been there, too.

THE INSECURITY CYCLE

Can you remember the last time you said something mean? If you really think about it, you can probably trace those words back to something hidden in your heart. When we feel hurt, pain, and insecurity, words just roll off our tongues, words we don't even take seriously. But they feel serious on the receiving end of things. And they hurt. And when a person feels hurt and insecure, he or she often uses mean words, too. It's a vicious cycle. If we want to stop it, though, it takes more than just being quiet. We also have to tackle the insecurity behind our words. Holding our tongues may help in the moment, but it can never fully heal our hearts.

Insecurity is sneaky. It's one of those embers we've been trying to stomp on, and it's probably the hardest one to put out. Know why? Because it can land on almost any part of our life and start to burn. Insecurity isn't picky. It will catch flame in any corner it can find. And while we are busy fighting the fires that threaten our body image, our materialism, and our popularity, insecurity can wander over and place itself right in the middle of our sentences and our lives without us even realizing it. Insecurity whispers this lie: "if you put her down, you will be lifted higher." At the root of a mean comment, you'll usually find the insecurities of someone's heart. So it might sound weird, but the best way for us to love others well is actually to believe truth about ourselves. When we put the fire of insecurity out in our hearts, it won't be so quick to spark into words that burn people we love.

MEAN IN TYPE

Unfortunately, social media has made it really easy to fan insecurity into flame. Somehow, it's easier to be mean when we're hiding behind technology. I'm sure we've all seen hateful words typed out in emails, Tweets, and texts. Things that we would *never* say to the faces of our classmates and friends become easy to throw out on the World Wide Web. Something about typing words on a screen can bring out some ugly things in our hearts. We feel invincible, it feels impersonal, and the other person seems unimportant. Somehow, handling words so carelessly seems okay with everyone, just as long as they're not spoken face to face. It breaks my heart. Because the idea that words are somehow less important because they're not being spoken out loud is one of the most deceiving lies of all.

My freshman year of high school was not so many years ago, but even then, we'd hardly heard of the word *cyberbullying*. It's a horrible reality that's spread like a wildfire over our generation. Words that are never even spoken out loud are breaking hearts, crushing spirits, and in some cases, even leading to suicide. Isn't this absolutely heartbreaking? It makes me want to hug every single girl who's been the victim of this awful, mean game.

#FACTCHAT

In September, 2013 a twelve-year-old girl in Florida killed herself by jumping from a tower at a concrete factory. She had struggled with deteriorating family relationships and depression for more than a year. But the sheriff's investigation of her death noted another key factor in her decision to take her own life. Cyberbullying. The girl had been tormented for several months on various social media outlets such as Kik, Ask.fm, Instagram, and Voxer. The sheriff's report included numerous hate-filled messages, such as "You should die. Why don't you go kill yourself" and "If you haven't killed yourself yet, would you please just die?"

- *Do you think the cyberbullies in this story are responsible for the girl's death? Why or why not?*
- *What causes someone to become a cyberbully? What kind of person tends to be their target?*
- *In general, how often do you see mean-spirited comments on the social media sites you use? Do you notice any "triggers" that cause mean comments to start being thrown around?*

(www.cbsnews.com/news/12-year-olds-suicide-spotlights -cyber-bullying-threat/)

As girls who are deciding not to let social media define us, can we draw a line in the sand right now? Let's not stand for this. Let's refuse to participate. And let's go one step further—let's come to the defense of those who are hurting. We can love them intentionally. We can use the power of *our* words to tell those girls the things their hearts are longing to hear: that they are valued and loved, that they are beautiful, and they are worth far more than they could ever imagine.

Maybe it sounds weird or intimidating to speak those words to a girl you don't really know. But let me ask you this: how often do you need to be reminded of those very same things yourself? We all long to hear that we're valued and loved. And when you start looking for people who need that kind of encouragement, it'll give you a lot of sympathy—and a lot of boldness. If you don't know what to say, try speaking Scripture. Send her a verse you've been inspired by in one of the previous chapters. Ask her to read Psalm 139. There's so much truth in the pages of Scripture; you don't have to come up with anything on your own. Just let her know that she's loved. Be the one who loves her. It could be revolutionary—for her and for you.

MEAN IN YOU

Has reading this chapter made you feel a little bit guilty? Maybe when it comes to being mean, you haven't just been watching from the sidelines. Maybe you've been the mean girl at times, throwing out words on social media that are not kind or loving or wise. You're not the only one—I've been there more times than I'd like to count. Let me remind you of this: when we choose meanness, we're usually hurting others because our own hearts are hurt or confused. And if we want to stop this cycle, we need a serious injection of truth into our hearts. They're hard truths when we hear them for the first time, but they are freeing truths once we accept them. And they stop the cycle of mean, which is something all of our hearts are longing for.

Here's the truth: Mean words reveal your heart's desire. But as we talked about earlier, that desire isn't usually about trying to hurt someone. You know what's really at the root of the problem? The desire to be "better than." You might find yourself feeling threatened by a girl's looks, grades, style, sense of humor, athletic ability—you name it. Something about her just makes you feel like you don't measure up. And the lies begin to whisper, "If you talk her down, you can take her place. Everyone will love you more. *You* will become the smartest, the prettiest, the most talented . . ." And you cave. You subtly (or maybe not so subtly) sneak a jab at her into your conversations. Maybe you question her integrity. Or you say something mean right to her face—whether it's true or not. If you've done stuff like that, join the club. We've all been there.

This kind of thing doesn't happen only with the words girls speak out loud. Cutting words can also fill up our screens as we type. And even though they're not spoken, they still hurt, don't they? Those silent words hold just as much weight whether we're speaking directly to the person or talking behind their back. We all know that a mean text followed by, "Oops, wrong person," can hurt just as much as a harsh text that was intentionally sent to you. Sometimes it hurts more. Words can cut through a screen right to the heart, so let's be girls who protect the hearts of others, not girls who push them around.

Now maybe you're reading this and thinking, *I know what comes next. You're going to tell me that tearing others down isn't going to build me up. I've heard it before.* Well, that's true. You don't need to tear other girls down so that you can measure up. But most of us already know that, and it doesn't stop the mean words from rolling off our tongues, does it? The lie we really need to fight is the idea that we don't measure up in the first place.

Ever used the word frenemy? *Webster's defines it as "one who pretends to be a friend but is actually an enemy." What does it say about the state of female relationships that we have this word in our vocabulary? #WhatDoYouThink?*

•••

ALWAYS COMPETING

Being a woman has become a competition of epic proportions. The world tells us that we have to fight to be the best. We've adopted the mentality of "there can only be one." One star athlete. One valedictorian. One pageant winner. One girl with the best style, funniest jokes, or nicest car. You get the idea. But our hearts were never built for this ranking system. The call to be "the best" implies that some of us are going to be "less than." And that line of thinking is the exact opposite of the truth we find in the Bible.

Throughout life, you'll encounter people who are different from you. They'll have different looks, different abilities, and different personalities. But guess what? Different doesn't mean better or worse. If you were exactly like someone else, one of you wouldn't even need to exist. God created every person individually, not on some mass-produced assembly line. Every hair on your head, every word that you speak, and every ability that you have was lovingly fashioned. I know you might not always feel this way, but you are never "less than." So in moments when you start feeling like someone different is "better" than you, tell your emotions the truth, and remember that the truth stays the same no matter how you feel. In Christ, you are enough. Let that truth win.

You know what happens when we start believing the truth about ourselves? The insecurities and comparisons lose their grip on our hearts. We no longer need to tear anyone else down. And instead of trying to be "more than" everyone else, we can find joy in our differences. We all have different talents, different strengths and weaknesses, different lives—but we're equally valued and loved by the One who made us. That's the truth. And it's freeing to realize that we don't need to compete anymore.

#FACTCHAT

Seven in ten teenage girls feel that they are not good enough or do not measure up in some way, according to a report issued by the Dove Self-Esteem Fund in 2008. Respondents' insecurities included looks, performance in school, or relationships with family and friends. Among the study's other findings: 75 percent of girls with low self-esteem admitted to engaging in negative behaviors such as cutting, bullying, drinking, and smoking.

- Why do you think so many girls feel inadequate and insecure? What feeds these insecurities?
- When girls view one another primarily as competitors, how does that shape their behavior toward one another?
- What would be different about "Girl World" if we saw one another primarily as fellow teammates or life travelers?
- What can girls do to stop feeding one another's insecurities?

(www.isacs.org/misc_files/SelfEsteem_Report%20-%20 Dove%20Campaign%20for%20Real%20Beauty.pdf)

Maybe you're on the other side of this whole equation, though. Maybe you're mean to someone because you think they really *are* "less than" you. Maybe you're allowing your words to be reckless because you believe that someone *doesn't* matter very much. Maybe you think she's weird. Or she's messed up. Or she's not as talented or pretty as you are.

Thinking that someone is less important than you is a lie of the most vicious kind. That girl who you don't think is pretty or smart or talented? Jesus created her. He loves her—so much that He died for her. And He's already defined her as beautiful and loved and precious in His sight. *You* don't get to define her. Remember all those truths we've been preaching to ourselves about God's unconditional love? They are just as true about others.

The world may tell us that certain people are more valuable than others. But let's not buy into that lie. God doesn't love some people more and others less, and neither should we. If you feel your heart holding another girl in low regard, pray that Jesus will give you eyes to see her the way that He does. When you start looking at her through God's eyes, I think you'll find that any desire to extend mean words to her will fade away.

MEAN NO MORE

Hopefully, we can all agree that it's time to stop the spread of mean, especially on social media. But sometimes it's hard to know just what mean is, isn't it? Sometimes mean is painfully obvious. But other times, it's just not. For example, starting a false rumor is wrong. Everybody knows that. But what if it's news that's true? Can you share it then? Maybe you're not trying to spread the rumor. You're just filling in a couple of your best friends on the latest drama. Is that mean?

133

Jesus knows that I like to walk the line. I've been known to ask questions like, "How much can I speed without getting a ticket?" and "Do you think it'd matter if I was five minutes late to class? Because I really need to get coffee first." So if I'm going to stay within the lines, someone needs to tell me exactly what to do. Like I said, Jesus gets that. And thankfully, He gives a pretty clear line for me to use when deciding what it's okay to talk about. Sometimes I feel as if Ephesians 4:29 was written right to me. "Don't let any foul words come out of your mouth. Only say what is helpful when it is needed for building up the community so that it benefits those who hear what you say." He doesn't really leave any gray area to play around in, does He?

God challenges us not to let "*any* foul words come out of our mouths." Any. That's a word I understand. And *foul* isn't restricted to obscene language or inappropriate jokes, although we should steer away from those, too. If life-giving words bring healing to our hearts and restore wholeness to broken places, then any words which do the opposite of that—they're foul. And we need to avoid them at all cost. Not letting *any* talk like this come out of our mouths means that the rumors stop with us. True or not isn't the scale we should weigh our words on. The question we always need to ask is "are these words kind or not?"

If the opener to that verse from Ephesians wasn't clear enough, there's a follow-up that makes things even more black and white. It goes on to say that we should speak *only* "what is helpful when it is needed for building up the community so that it benefits those who hear what you say." There's no getting around Jesus's point from here on out. If it doesn't build others up, we shouldn't say it.

But what does it mean to build someone up "when it is needed"? Well, that phrase implies that we know what they need. And to know what someone needs, we have to know them, care about them, do life alongside of them. Basically, the best way we can know how to encourage people is to intentionally love them and serve them. That way, if one of them is discouraged, we'll know, and we can be there with encouraging words and a hug or a cup of coffee. (Is coffee a love language? I really think so.) Obeying this verse means that we have to get to know people, and then we have to love them. No small task. But it's worth it.

REAL LIFE LOVE

Can social media help with this process of knowing and loving people? In some ways, maybe. But we have to be careful. Following people on social media and knowing them in real life are nothing alike. I found this out when I jumped into the world of Instagram.

There's a girl I went to college with who was an Instagram legend. She had thousands of followers. Her captions were witty and poetic, and they accompanied pictures of international travel, great fashion, and exciting adventures. I followed her on Instagram because everyone did. And I secretly thought that I would be intimidated to meet this girl with the perfect life. She was just way cooler than I was. And that was that. Until one day, I ran into her at a coffee shop.

We ended up grabbing a table and chatting, and after about ten minutes, I realized something. All that time I'd spent wanting her life, feeling intimidated by her put-togetherness, and wondering if my life looked as cool as hers was a waste. The girl sitting across the table from me was shy and nervous and worried what I thought of her. What I thought of *her*! I falsely believed that she was queen of the Insta-world because it looked that way on my newsfeed. But filters and captions can never drown out insecurity in real life. Someone's life can look perfect online and still feel really empty.

That experience taught me that I needed to love this girl in real life. Everyone loved her pictures and her words—but she needed a real-life friend who cared about her and loved her. She and I are still friends. And I've tried my best to be the kind of friend who cares more about her heart than about where she's just flown in from. I've come to love her because of who she is, not because of who she knows and what she looks like. Was it easier to just admire her on Instagram? Yes, for sure. But am I learning a lot more through knowing her as a person? Absolutely.

How many people could you encourage with positive comments on social media in just ten minutes?
#GiveItATry

●●●

I'm learning not to let people spark my envy online, but I've also encountered people who do the exact opposite—they spark my temper. Some people are just annoying on social media, aren't they? But we're called to love even the people who get under our skin. Their online presence is just the surface. We have to dig deep, care until it hurts, and love people for who they really are—even if they do annoy us at times. Retweets and followers can't define our feelings about people. We have to decide that they are worth loving. And then we have to build them up according to what they need.

You know what's most exciting about using our words to love like this? Just check out the end of the Ephesians verse we've been studying: It says "so that it benefits those who hear what you say." It's like Jesus knew Twitter was going to be a thing thousands of years down the road. (Which, of course, He did.) This is my favorite part of the verse because it applies so clearly to social media.

When we consistently speak life and encouragement into the lives of those around us, it benefits *the other people* who observe it. No one has ever had a bigger audience than we do, right now, because of social media. With more people listening to us, we can show the love of Jesus to more people. Math has never been my strong suit, but I know that's a good equation. So let's build others up. Let's speak kindness and truth and love. You never know who will be listening in.

This whole topic of speaking kind words probably hasn't been new to you. But I hope you've found new motivation for choosing those kind words. So much of our reckless language is rooted in lies and insecurities, and I'm praying you have a newfound passion to fight against those lies. Don't you think it's time we take back our identity as loved daughters of the Lord? Let's declare that life-giving truth to every girl we know.

As we close out the conversation, hold onto these words from Proverbs 16:24: "Pleasant words are flowing honey, / sweet to the taste and healing to the bones." As girls who are following the example of Jesus, we can bring honey to the souls of those who've been hurt by lies. When we speak the truth boldly, we can help others to feel the sweetness of Jesus' love. And that's worth getting on social media to proclaim any day.

Don't let any foul words come out of your mouth. Only say what is helpful when it is needed for building up the community so that it benefits those who hear what you say.
—Ephesians 4:29

IDENTITY: TAKING IT BACK

1. When are you the most likely to be reckless with your words? We all have certain situations that cause our filter to disappear. Figure out what causes you to be careless with the words you say or type. Ask God to help you guard yourself when those triggers appear.

2. Pick a few people that you will intentionally encourage this week. Send them a kind word. It could be a text, a wall post, or even a handwritten note. You never know what a difference you could be making in their hearts.

REDEEMING OUR TIME (& OUR TWEETS)

It's hard to look in the mirror and see that we've believed lies, especially when those lies have caused us to question who we really are. We've fought hard against the lies of comparison, materialism, popularity, body image, and reckless words. But we've also experienced joy as we learned to defeat those lies and declare the truth. Hard, but filled with joy: that's the journey we've been through in this book. It also sounds a lot like the way we journey through life.

And now we get to the fun part.

We've learned all about what *not* to believe, and why. Now we get to talk about what we can do instead. We *can* redeem our time on social media and make it something great. We *can* walk with confidence into the places that used to drag us down. And now that we understand the truth about whose we are, we *can* share that good news with the hurting hearts around us.

Yes, social media can fan little lies into dangerous flames. But now we know how to fight those flames. Since the fires have been extinguished in our own hearts, let's start carrying buckets of water to the girls who need it most. We are free. Let's use that freedom to tell everyone else that they're loved, valued, and beautiful, too.

Are you ready?

Chapter 10

BREAKING THE CYCLE

Learning to Be Instead of Do

We've been tackling struggle after struggle as we've walked through these chapters. You might be a little tired. And that's OK. Sometimes it takes all the emotional strength we have to trek through the lies, much less to find where those lies have been burning away at our identities. And then we have to somehow find energy to pour truth on those fires until they sizzle and crackle into nothing. It's really hard work.

Hopefully, the challenges in this book haven't just left you tired, though. I hope that you're starting to feel a sliver of hope in your heart. Actually, I want you to feel way more than a sliver. I hope your heart is bursting with joy—knowing that you are fully known and still fully loved. I hope you're walking with an extra spring in your step, confident that you're beautiful simply because Jesus says so. And I hope you look in the mirror and smile because you know you're valuable regardless of what happens on Twitter today.

I hope you feel free, because if you are in Christ, you *are* free.

You've fought hard to believe in that freedom. And you know what I think should come next? Rest! Rest in the truth. Rest in the freedom. Rest in Jesus' love. It's the only thing that will satisfy and restore you.

#FACTCHAT

In August 2014, the American Academy of Pediatrics issued a recommendation that middle and high schools delay start times to 8:30 a.m. so teens could have more sleeping time.
(www.aap.org/en-us/about-the-aap/aap-press-room/
Pages/Let-Them-Sleep-AAP-Recommends-Delaying-Start
-Times-of-Middle-and-High-Schools-to-Combat-Teen-Sleep
-Deprivation.aspx)

TAKE A BREAK!

Ever curl up with a good book or magazine on a lazy afternoon? There's nothing better when you're resting than a good story. Lucky for you, I've got a good one.

As I shared earlier, I got saved when I was pretty young. Salvation means that sin no longer has to be your master. Those chains are broken; you're free. And so was I. But as I got older and the lies of the world got louder, I started living as though sin *was* still in charge. Even though my chains were broken off and I didn't have to stay under them anymore, I continued to tangle myself up in them.

For me, that meant I still let voices tell me that I had to be good at things to be good enough. Jesus had already set my value, but I kept trying to make myself valuable in the eyes of everyone else. I still let ugly things like pride and anger rule in my heart—and they grew into tiring burdens. Life felt heavy and I felt stuck, even though I knew I was *supposed* to be free.

Does that story resonate with you? Maybe that's how you were feeling before you picked up this book. The reason I wrote this book in the first place is because I see so many girls tangled in these chains, even girls who I know have embraced God's gift of freedom and salvation. It breaks my heart—because my heart remembers just how painful it is to carry that heavy load. Thankfully, my story didn't end there. And yours doesn't have to either.

NO MORE HEAVY LIFTING

A few years ago, my eyes were opened to all these chains weighing me down. I recognized this whole stolen identity situation for the first time. I realized how much I'd let myself be deceived. Have you heard about the "fight or flight" response? Well, I fought. I was mad that I'd believed lies for so long. And I decided to study the Bible and spend time in prayer to combat them.

As I learned how to shake those chains of lies off of my heart, I felt so much joy that I literally couldn't contain it. A weight had been lifted from my soul, and I just wanted to use my newfound freedom to serve Jesus in any way I could. I started attending a Bible study and leading another one. I lead worship for multiple events each week. I started blogging. I met with countless girls for dinner or coffee and told them about what Jesus had done for me. I blew up social media with happy sentences that ended in #blessed. And I did it all with great intentions. I was just so excited!

When I look back at that season, I laugh. And shake my head. Because in hindsight I can see the imminent disaster on the horizon from a mile away. Want to guess what happened?

I burned out.

Even in the midst of my excitement, I started feeling tired. Tired turned into exhausted. My joy diminished, and the things I had loved doing a few short months ago turned into tasks that I dreaded. I just didn't have energy for them anymore. I had overcommitted in a big way, and the comedown was just as big.

At the time, I didn't understand why I couldn't just feel like the Energizer bunny. Everything I was doing was for Jesus. Because I was free! So why would ministry make me feel so tired and burdened again?

You know what? I'd missed the point. Jesus didn't set me free to do a bunch of things. He set me free so that I could finally rest. But I didn't know how to do that. I got so caught up in doing things *for* Jesus that I didn't leave any time to spend *with* Him. I was trying to change the whole world on my own strength, and I failed miserably. Something had to change.

#FACTCHAT
In her 2007 book titled The Overachievers, *Alexandra Robbins studies the trend of overscheduled and overstressed teenagers that is prevalent among many*

American high schools. Included in the book's description are these words: "High school isn't what it used to be. With record numbers of students competing fiercely to get into college, schools are no longer primarily places of learning. They're dog-eat-dog battlegrounds in which kids must set aside interests and passions in order to strategize over how to game the system. In this increasingly stressful environment, kids aren't defined by their character or hunger for knowledge, but by often arbitrary scores and statistics."

- Does this description sound like your own school experience? Why or why not?
- How many different roles (extracurricular activities, jobs, church/community involvement, and so on) are you balancing in your life right now? Does it feel like a healthy balance? Why or why not?
- What are some of the "side effects" you notice in a teenager culture that encourages overachieving?
- Why is taking a break important? Do you think teens rest often enough?

THE JOY OF BEING

I spent the next few months doing—well, not much. From the outside, it probably looked like I was doing a whole lot of nothing. But inside, I was learning how to rest in the Lord for the very first time. Before I found freedom, I was always fighting to get approval from people for my looks, my talents, and my personality. After I embraced freedom, I was still fighting. Only now I was fighting to do enough, say enough, be enough—for Jesus. Notice the subtle little lie there? There's the catch: I don't have to *do* anything at all. Jesus doesn't love me because of anything I do. He loves me because of who I *am*—His creation. He loves me because He is good, and it's in His nature to love—even when I don't deserve it.

My journey to finding freedom from sin was important. But my journey to finding rest was every bit as crucial to my soul. Both have set me free from the burden of *doing* everything and helped me find joy in just being loved by Jesus.

I hope you're feeling a little lighter these days, a little freer as you've let go of the lies social media can lay on your heart. Freedom brings joy, and I hope you feel like celebrating. You should! Just remember that your enthusiasm over this new freedom doesn't have to lead to overcommitting and burning out. Learn to *be* with Jesus before you try to go out and *do* everything for Him. The truth is He doesn't need us to do anything for Him. He loves it when our hearts are willing to serve Him, and He will always open doors for us to do that. But we don't need to carry the weight of doing things for Jesus. He's God. He's got it handled.

So love Jesus. Lean into Him. Rest in Him. I've seen firsthand how He'll lead you if you just keep your eyes on Him. In fact, that's exactly what Hebrews 12:1-2 tells us: "So then let's also run the race that is laid out in front of us, since we have such a great cloud of witnesses surrounding us. Let's throw off any extra baggage, get rid of the sin that trips us up, and fix our eyes on Jesus, faith's pioneer and perfecter." The world is watching us. So should we throw off those chains that used to keep us from freedom? Absolutely!

But did you notice the next step? It's not to fix the world. It's to fix our eyes on Jesus. So take a deep breath, and rest.

If you were forced to choose, what would you pick: going out and doing things for God or staying put and being with Him (prayer, Bible study, journaling, and so on)? #WhatDoYouThink?

• • •

TAKING A BREAK

Now for the hard part of resting. What I'm about to say might make you a little nervous. That's okay. It was a little hard for me to take my own advice, too. But let me ask you this: After fighting a huge forest fire, would you just sit down in the woods and hang out, hoping another fire doesn't spring up? Of course not. You'd go home. You'd nurse your wounds. You'd need to rest. And since the fires we've been fighting are on social media—I think it makes sense to leave that online forest for a while.

Now before you throw this book across the room, let me say this: I'm *not* advocating that you run away from social media forever. There's a big difference between deleting all your accounts for all time and choosing to step back and rest for a bit. The first idea is ridiculous—even I would throw the book for that one. The second idea is restorative.

You know what tends to happen when social media has been the source of lies in your life? Once you're free from those lies, you'll want to get back online and preach the truth. And that's actually a great idea. But don't rush it. Why? Because you need to spend some time *in* the truth before you proclaim it. Lies are powerful things. And if you jump back into the social media world right away, you might get sucked right back into the lies and forget the truth. That's dangerous.

Here's an even sneakier, but every bit as dangerous, scenario: you might start finding your worth in how many people you are reaching with the truth. If you Tweet a Bible verse, and no one favorites it, you're totally justified in your anger, right? . . . Well, nope.

Sharing truth on social media can be a great ministry. But if you start building your identity on the statements you make about Jesus, you've defeated the whole purpose of finding freedom in the first place. Your identity is not in your ministry; your identity is in your Savior. I admit I got confused about that for a while. It's one of the hardest lies to defeat because it looks so promising on the outside. And most people aren't going to call you out on it. "Hey, you should stop caring about your ministry so much," just doesn't have a nice ring to it, does it?

But real community is honest. And since we're all a part of this lie-fighting community together, I'll call you out on it. Even though it's a noble goal, your identity can't be based on a social media ministry. To be honest, I struggled with this identity simply because I didn't rest from social media. And I would hate for you to do the same thing. Learn from my failures. Hop off social media for a little while and be with the One who created your heart and is jealous for it.

Too hard to quit cold turkey? What if you logged off two hours more each day over the course of two weeks—building up to two final days that would be social-media free? #GiveItATry

● ● ●

I can't tell you exactly what your break from social media should look like. I don't know if you need a week, two weeks, or a month. I *would* say that twenty-four hours is not enough. Your heart needs to be refocused, and that doesn't happen overnight. Maybe you need to tell people you're taking a break or maybe you just silently slip away for a while. Maybe you need a break from texting or maybe deleting your apps will be enough. I can't tell you, because I don't know where your heart is in this moment. But the beautiful thing is Jesus does.

If you need help figuring out what your season of rest should look like, ask! James 1:5 says, "If any of you lacks wisdom, you should ask God, who gives generously to all without finding fault, and it will be given to you" (NIV). Isn't that incredible? I don't know about you, but I lack wisdom at times. And to find it, I need to step away from the chatter of social media and rest in Jesus. I'm learning to ask Him for a big dosage of wisdom in my life and then stay away from the noise long enough to hear His response. God has more wisdom than we can fathom, and He gives it *generously* without judging us in any way. Lies continue to fight for my heart. The difference? Now I know where to turn.

I've decided to rest and seek Jesus every time the seasons change outside. I'm finding that I need Him more and more in each new season of my heart. That's right—four social media fasts every year. They don't all look exactly alike, but they all involve me logging off my accounts and tuning in to the truth. I won't lie; it's really hard. I love my Twitter feed almost as much I love my morning coffee. But every time, I walk away from those seasons of rest feeling more loved by my Jesus and ready to take that love to social media with a new fire in my bones.

So does *your* heart ever feel exhausted and worn? When it does, let the words of Jesus in Matthew 11:28 wash over your soul: "Come to me, all you who are struggling hard and carrying heavy loads, and I will give you rest." A heart at rest. Now that's something worth logging off for, isn't it?

So then let's also run the race that is laid out in front of us, since we have such a great cloud of witnesses surrounding us. Let's throw off any extra baggage, get rid of the sin that trips us up, and fix our eyes on Jesus, faith's pioneer and perfecter. He endured the cross, ignoring the shame, for the sake of the joy that was laid out in front of him, and sat down at the right side of God's throne.
—Hebrews 12:1-2

IDENTITY: TAKING IT BACK

Time to make an action plan. How are you going to rest from social media? Spend time praying and asking Jesus to give you the details. How long will you stay off social media? What sites will you avoid? What do you need to focus on instead during this time? Write it out. And then look at it every day. There's an awesome season of restoration right around the corner. You can do it. Get ready. Get rested.

Chapter 11

GONE VIRAL

An Identity Revolution

Have you ever wished you'd just skipped the last chapter of a book? So often, the conclusion is just a bunch of paragraphs that are vague and encouraging. They leave you a little bit uplifted but mostly confused. And since there's no direction on how to apply it all to real life, you just close the book and slide it back onto the shelf to collect dust.

I hate last chapters like that. So you know what? I'm not going to give you a final chapter.

These are the last few pages of the book, yes. But I'd prefer to consider this the opening chapter of a new story—*your* story. It might not be typed out like this, but your story is worth telling. Through the pages you've turned in this book, you've fought battles, learned to believe truth, and taken some time to rest. Now, I'm sending you to the front lines.

The freedom you've found is just way too good to keep to yourself. I don't want it to collect dust on the shelf beside all those books with boring conclusions. I know you'll put this book on your shelf, but please don't lay your freedom down beside it. Carry the truth with you. In a world filled with lies, you'll need it every day.

So how do you actually do that? How can you carry truth and keep joy alive? How can you kick those lies to the floor again and again? Well, I'm going to offer some practical suggestions. But only you can put them into action. Vague conclusions, as frustrating as they are, keep you comfortable. They allow you to just think about what you read for a couple of days and then walk on, unchanged. Not this time. I care way too much about your heart to leave you stranded without an action plan. So here are a few ideas to help you enjoy social media without letting it steal your identity.

KEEP THE TRUTH WITH YOU

You are beautiful, valued, and loved. I don't know how many times I've written those words in this book. But they aren't true because *I* said them. They're true because Jesus says so. There's nothing more important than the truth in the Bible. So if you only choose to follow one of my suggestions, make it this one.

Of course, you can't just carry the entire Bible around with you all the time. It's not always convenient, even if you have the app on your phone. Even better than a Bible in our hands is holding the word our hearts. If you *know* the truth like the back of your hand, then you can speak it when those lies start to whisper again.

Did you notice something at the end of every chapter? There was a verse there—truth from God's word to fight each specific lie. Here's my suggestion: memorize those verses. That might sound hard. But I bet if you're anything like me, you know the words to hundreds of songs. So if you put your mind to it, I know you can do it. Here they are, all in one place.

#FACTCHAT

On average, a Bible chapter is twenty-six verses long. That means if you memorized one verse per day, you could have fourteen chapters memorized in a year.

Examine me, God! Look at my heart!
Put me to the test! Know my anxious thoughts!
Look to see if there is any idolatrous way in me,
then lead me on the eternal path!
—Psalm 139:23-24

"Then you will know the truth, and the truth will set you free."
—John 8:32

I give thanks to you that I was marvelously set apart.
Your works are wonderful—I know that very well.
—Psalm 139:14

Don't try to make yourselves beautiful on the outside, with stylish hair or by wearing gold jewelry or fine clothes. Instead, make

yourselves beautiful on the inside, in your hearts, with the endur-
ing quality of a gentle, peaceful spirit. This type of beauty is very
precious in God's eyes.
—1 Peter 3:3-4

Godliness is a great source of profit when it is combined with being
happy with what you already have.
—1 Timothy 6:6

Let the words of my mouth
and the meditations of my heart
be pleasing to you,
LORD, my rock and my redeemer.
—Psalm 19:14

Wisdom that comes from heaven is first of all pure; then peace-
loving, considerate, submissive, full of mercy and good fruit,
impartial and sincere.
—James 3:17 (NIV)

Your word is a lamp before my feet
and a light for my journey.
—Psalm 119:105

Don't let any foul words come out of your mouth. Only say what is
helpful when it is needed for building up the community so that it
benefits those who hear what you say.
—Ephesians 4:29

So then let's also run the race that is laid out in front of us, since we have such a great cloud of witnesses surrounding us. Let's throw off any extra baggage, get rid of the sin that trips us up, and fix our eyes on Jesus, faith's pioneer and perfecter. He endured the cross, ignoring the shame, for the sake of the joy that was laid out in front of him, and sat down at the right side of God's throne.
—Hebrews 12:1-2

He said to them, "Go into the whole world and proclaim the good news to every creature."
—Mark 16:15

JOURNAL

Maybe, like me, you have dozens of journals stacked in the corner of your room. Or maybe you've never kept a journal in your whole life. Either way, I'd encourage you to spend some time writing about the truth. I'm not asking you to chronicle what you had for lunch or if your socks matched today. We don't need to journal so we can remember what our days looked like. (Although if you want to, go for it!) We need to journal because Jesus is faithful.

Of course, you aren't sinning if you choose not to write down your journey through freedom. It's not required. But I find that I need to journal, because I forget. I forget that when I pray for things—even crazy, bold, huge things—Jesus answers. I forget that I had really hard days, and He was faithful. I forget that I received unexpected blessings. And when I forget, I start to resent the bad days and take the good ones for granted. Looking back over my journals reminds me of just how good Jesus is to me. It's my own personal reminder of truth, day in and day out.

There have also been seasons of my life when I stopped journaling. I just got busy or it got tiring. And looking back, it's one of my biggest regrets. Being able to read, in my own words, about the times I've grown closer to Jesus is the coolest gift I've given myself.

Not sure what to say in a journal? That's okay. There's no perfect formula. Journal about what you read in the Bible. Write out those verses you're trying to memorize. (I've found that writing them down really helps me remember.) Write down what you're praying for—and then go back and write down when your prayers get answered. Write about your really hard days and your really good ones. Just write. You will look back and see that Jesus was fighting for you every single day.

Do you have a tablet or smartphone that travels with you everywhere? What if you made it a habit to journal quick notes on your device when you notice God throughout your day? #GiveItATry

•••

GO VIRAL

After the previous chapter, hopefully you hopped off social media for a bit. Maybe you started doing some memorizing or journaling. But the more you learn to rest in the truth, the more excited you'll be to get back on social media and *tell the world.* And, girl, you should! Freedom changes everything. Knowing who you are changes everything. *Jesus* changes everything. Can you imagine if everyone understood that?

There would be an identity revolution.

I'm a big dreamer, because I serve a big God. And so I've been praying that this revolution will happen. We've seen it happen before: stuff goes viral all the time. (My personal favorites are usually videos of people saying ridiculous things after they get their wisdom teeth out.) If videos of stunts gone wrong and funny animals can be shared with millions of people, why can't the most important message of all time do the same thing?

#FACTCHAT

How many Americans have dumped ice-cold water over their heads? Quite a few—thanks to the Ice Bucket Challenge. Participants—including well-known movie stars, athletes, and politicians—dumped ice water over their heads in an effort to raise money and awareness for ALS research, posted videos of the event, and then challenged others to do the same. The Ice Bucket Challenge went viral on social media in mid-2014, with more than 1.2 million Facebook videos being posted from June through August, and over 2 million Twitter references during just three weeks in late July-early August. The ALS Association reported that over $100 million of additional funding was raised due to the publicity.

- *What are some other examples of videos/causes that have gone viral on social media?*
- *In what ways is the "going viral" effect a good thing? In what ways can it be a bad thing?*
- *What are some messages/ideas that you wish could go viral in social media?*
- *Brainstorm some creative ways that Christians could try to go viral on social media: Is there on idea you could try? (http://en.wikipedia.org/wiki/Ice_Bucket_Challenge)*

We hold the message that hearts are longing for. And we have the biggest audience of any generation, ever. Let's not throw this advantage away. People are listening to us. So let's be a force of encouragement. Let's be kind. Speak truth. Speak freedom. Speak the gospel. It'll be the opposite of what most of social media is saying. So it'll get attention. But don't hear me wrong here: I'm not asking anyone to go preach. I'm asking you to fall so in love with Jesus that you can't help but spill out that love everywhere. Even on Twitter, Facebook, and Instagram.

Let's start an identity revolution. You in?

May His love go viral.

He said to them, "Go into the whole world and proclaim the good news to every creature."
—Mark 16:15

IDENTITY: TAKING IT BACK

1. Psalm 119:11 says, "I have hidden your word in my heart / that I might not sin against you" (NIV). The Bible is the best plan we could ever create when it comes to defeating lies. So how are you going to memorize Bible verses? Try writing them out. Tape them on your mirror. Learn them with a friend. Or come up with a creative idea of your own to hold truth deep in your heart.

2. Do you know someone who needs to hear the truth about who they are? Is it your mom, sister, friend, classmate, coworker? Start praying for them, every day. And pray that Jesus would give you opportunities to share that they are loved, beautiful, and valued—and that that Jesus came to set them free. I can't wait to hear about the ways Jesus works when you share the good news!

ACKNOWLEDGMENTS

Mom and Dad: Thanks for teaching me who I am in Christ through every season, and for believing in this book even before I did. This message never would have existed without you both. If all the parents in the world were standing on a stage, I'd pick you every time.

My small group girls: Thanks for letting me into your world so that we can walk through life and toward Jesus together. You guys have shaped my heart in ways you'll never know, and I love you all like crazy!

Pamela Clements and the Abingdon Press team: Thank you for taking a crazy chance on me and walking me through the world of publishing. Your dreams for this book blew me away from day one, and I am so thankful for every single minute that you've devoted to making this message a reality.

Jana Burson: You are editor extraordinaire—thanks for making me sound more like myself and for reworking methods without changing the message. So thankful for you!

Acknowledgments

To my friends and family who supported my crazy idea to write a book: THANK YOU. I could fill up page after page with the ways you all made this a reality. You listened while I shared my heart and read draft after draft to you. You stayed friends with me even when I disappeared into my writing cave for weeks on end. You prayed for and with me over every word. You didn't give up, even when I wanted to. I couldn't ask for people who love me better.

To you, readers: Thank you for letting me share my heart with you. Thank you for wanting to know where your identity lies. I feel like we're friends already, especially if you made it to the end of these acknowledgements. Let's grab coffee sometime. :)

To Jesus: You are at the roots of this book, and You are the miracle worker who opened doors every step of the way. Thank You for giving me this message. Thank You for not letting me share it until the time was right. I am thankful to You for a million things beyond these pages. May every word of this book point people straight to You.

WHEN PAIN RUNS DEEP

Hi, sister. I'm so glad you've taken the time to meet me in the back of this book with all your hurts and scars. I already know that you are brave for turning to this page. And I already know that you are loved.

Some chapters of this book mention the lighthearted side of the struggles we face as girls. That isn't intended to make light of the very real and painful struggles that some of you face. We may joke about braids and boys, but that might seem ridiculous in light of the pain you're feeling right now. Problems, big and small, come from the lies we believe about ourselves. I wish I could give you a quick formula to make it all better. But there's no cookie-cutter solution for all these problems. What I can do is offer some honest conversation about the pain you might be feeling, pain that goes much deeper than hairstyles or jewelry preferences.

TO MY FRIENDS WITH AN EATING DISORDER

I know you want to feel beautiful. I know because I feel that desire, too. It's rooted deep in our souls. I haven't struggled with anorexia or bulimia, but I have struggled to be content with my body, my weight, and my beauty. I won't pretend to know the pain you go through as you try to reach your target weight, the point where you believe you will finally be thin enough. But I can promise you that Jesus has felt deep physical pain, and He is walking by your side through your experience. He created you, and He thinks you are absolutely flawless. No number on a scale could ever change the depth of His love for you or the intensity of your beauty in His eyes. I'm praying that your heart will begin to believe that truth. I want you to know that you are *already enough* in God's eyes.

I also realize that sometimes words are not enough to break the cycle of an eating disorder. Do you long to be free from the chains anorexia and bulimia have put around you? If you'd like to get some practical help, here are some resources to give you something solid to hold on to. I pray that they'll help pull you out of the pain and pressure you've been living under.

For more information, contact: Eating Disorders Awareness and Prevention: 1-800-931-2237

National Association of Anorexia Nervosa and Associated Disorders: 1-847-831-3438

TO MY FRIENDS WHO ARE INVOLVED IN SELF-HARM

Whether you're cutting, burning yourself, or causing another kind of harm to your body, I am deeply sorry that you have unbearable pain in your heart. I haven't struggled with self-harm, but I have definitely struggled with pain inside that I just didn't know how to handle. I've felt helpless and out of control, and I remember just how hard it was to get past that in my life.

It's OK to have pain. You don't have to hide the fact that you're hurting. In fact, hiding pain inside like it's a secret can sometimes just make things hurt more. I don't know what kind of pain you're experiencing, but Jesus does. He has been walking beside you for every single step, and when you hurt, so does He. He created you and loves you, and His heart is broken when you are suffering. Can you grab on to that truth? I hope your heart will start believing that He understands you, even in your darkest moments.

I know that words, even the most encouraging ones, sometimes aren't enough to break a cycle that has served as an outlet for your pain for so long. I would love for you to check out these practical ways to understand and express your pain in different ways—ways that don't harm your body. Sweet friend, I want you to know that Jesus thinks you are beautiful, even in the middle of all your hurt and pain and scars. He loves you, and I'm praying that you'll feel that love in a new way today.

For further reading or help, visit:

Self Abuse Finally Ends: www.selfinjury.com

"The Gospel of Grace for Women Who Self-Injure," www .christianitytoday.com/women/2011/february/gospel-of-grace -for-women-who-self-injure.html?paging=off

Appendix 2

GRACE

Hey, friend! The story of God's grace gets me more excited than anything else in the whole world. And I'm thrilled that you want to learn more about it. If you want the whole story, you'll want to read the Bible for yourself. But here's a brief overview of what it's all about. Let's dive right in.

In the very beginning, God created. He spoke the whole universe into existence, from the most enormous constellations to the tiniest microscopic cells. It's all His handiwork—and so are we. He created man and woman, gave them a garden to live in and take care of, and loved them endlessly. From the beginning, His heart was to be in community with them.

But Adam and Eve, the first humans, disobeyed the one rule God had given them in the garden. They ate fruit from the only tree they were commanded not to. Why? Because Satan and his lies deceived them. He told them God was trying to keep them from something good, that they would be wiser if they ate this fruit. Funny how from the very beginning, problems always start when we believe lies instead of standing on the truth.

Adam and Eve bought into Satan's lie. And it led them right into sin—disobedience of God. And that's when humanity became separated from God. Of course, God didn't love Adam and Eve any less because they messed up. But in His holiness, He had to be separate from their sin.

(If you'd like to study the story of creation and how humans messed up, you can read Genesis 1–3 in the Bible. It's at the very beginning.)

To make a very long story short, for thousands of years after that, humanity just continued to sin. They actually got stuck in a cycle. They'd rebel against God, experience punishment, come back to God in desperation, get rescued and comfortable, and then rebel all over again. That pattern is woven throughout the entire Old Testament. Always yearning to be in relationship with people, God set up a system of animal sacrifices to temporarily pay the penalty for His people's sins. But He had something much bigger and much more drastic in store. Something that would bridge the gap between our sinfulness and His holiness permanently.

Only perfect blood could cover the weight of all our sins and restore us to our Creator. So God sent His perfect Son, Jesus, to the earth as a baby. Can you believe that? The God who created humans was willing to come to earth and live as one. Jesus was 100 percent God—He was holy and without sin. But He was also 100 percent human. He could relate to us in our humanity, to the temptations we face and the trials we endure. It's hard to wrap our minds around the truth of Jesus being both God and human—it defies human logic. We just have to trust that God is capable of it. I, for one, am very thankful that He is.

So what came next? Jesus grew up. He loved sinners and started preaching something different from what the leaders wanted people to believe. He preached the truth. And some people hated the truth. Those people ultimately got Jesus sentenced to death on a Roman cross. But unlike the temporary animal sacrifices of the Old Testament, Jesus' sinless life and sacrificial death provided the ultimate sacrifice for our sins. Our debt was paid.

Thankfully, God's story doesn't end there. After three days, Jesus rose from the dead. He's God—so He can do that! Nothing is impossible for God. Jesus rose to life and went back to heaven, and He's ruling there even now. When we believe that all of this is true and choose to surrender to Him, we're guaranteed a spot in heaven with Him for all of eternity. We won't have to spend forever in hell, separated from the God who loves us.

Even though "all have sinned and fallen short of God's glory" (Romans 3:23), Christ died for us "while we were still sinners" (Romans 5:8). Maybe that sounds crazy to you. You know what? It *is* crazy that a perfect and powerful God would care enough about our messed up lives to rescue us and draw us back into community with Him. But it's true. And you want to know why He does it? *Because He loves us.* And God's love led to a grace like no one has ever seen.

What do we have to do to get this ridiculous amount of grace poured out on us? Just receive it. Let it cover our sins past, present, and future. That's it. We don't have to change ourselves, clean up, fix our problems, or shake free from sin first. (Which is good, because we can't do any of that on our own anyway.) We just come to Jesus. We give Him our burdens and our sins and we surrender it all. He takes our mess; we get His love in return. It's too good to make sense to our imperfect minds, and yet it's the truest thing in the world. I know it's true because I've experienced it. I've felt the chains of sin being broken and my burdens being lifted. And now my soul is free. My heart is joyful. My worth is secure.

Do you long for those things in your life?

If you've never trusted Jesus with your life, there's never been a more perfect moment than this one. He loves you more than you could ever understand. And you can find rest in that boundless love. It's amazing. If you want to accept this grace and salvation in your life, just take a moment to pray to God, right now. Maybe you'll want to say something like this:

> God, I know I'm a sinner. My life is really messed up, and I know I can't fix it on my own. But I also believe that You can. Thank you for dying so that I can be loved by You. I believe that You died, You rose again, and that Your grace is what I'm missing. I give my life to You. I'm surrendering. I know that I still have some messes to work through, but I know Your love is strong enough to change me from the inside out. I'm ready. I surrender. Thank You for this beautiful thing called grace. Amen.

A prayer alone is not what saves you. Believing in Jesus and surrendering your life to His love and grace is what saves you. If you just prayed and believed those words, then it's time to celebrate because you just crossed from death to life. This is the beginning of an incredible journey for you—one that'll last your whole life and even into eternity. I'm so excited to see how God shows up and shows off in your life. Hang on, sister. Things are about to get good.

Hi! I'm **Jessica Fralin**. On any given day, you can find me tucked into a quiet corner with a good book or typing my way through life on JessicaFralin.com. It means the world to me that you picked up this book. If you're like me, you'll grab a cup of coffee and nestle in, learning who you are—and why it matters—especially when it comes to social media.

Want More?

Chat with us at
Twubs.com/IdentityRevolution

@ JessicaFralin

#FACTCHAT

#GIVEITATRY

join the
#IdentityRevolution
take back what social media
has #stolen

#WHATDOYOUTHINK